A Primer on Wireless Technology and IoT Basics

Authored by

Mamatha Balachandra & Balachandra Muniyal

School of Computer Engineering
Manipal Institute of Technology
Manipal Academy of Higher Education
Udupi, Karnataka, India

A Primer on Wireless Technology and IoT Basics

Authors: Mamatha Balachandra and Balachandra Muniyal

ISBN (Online): 979-8-89881-012-2

ISBN (Print): 979-8-89881-013-9

ISBN (Paperback): 979-8-89881-014-6

Published by Bentham Science Publishers Pte. Ltd. Singapore, in collaboration with Eureka Conferences, USA. All Rights Reserved.

First published in 2025.

need for a court order if at any point you breach any terms of this License Agreement. In no event will any delay or failure by Bentham Science Publishers in enforcing your compliance with this License Agreement constitute a waiver of any of its rights.

3. You acknowledge that you have read this License Agreement, and agree to be bound by its terms and conditions. To the extent that any other terms and conditions presented on any website of Bentham Science Publishers conflict with, or are inconsistent with, the terms and conditions set out in this License Agreement, you acknowledge that the terms and conditions set out in this License Agreement shall prevail.

Bentham Science Publishers Pte. Ltd.
No. 9 Raffles Place
Office No. 26-01
Singapore 048619
Singapore
Email: subscriptions@benthamscience.net

CONTENTS

FOREWORD

Wireless Communication introduced a paradigm shift in long-distance communication. With the success of landline telephone networks as well as computer/data networks, the need for mobile telephone networks was felt. This requirement was materialized with the commercialization of cellular communication networks. It was realized that wireless networks without infrastructure are necessarily required in many applications, including military communications. Further, the success of cellular networks led to other wireless sensor networks. Short and medium-range wireless networks, such as WiFi networks and wireless personal area networks, were materialized, providing ubiquitous communication. This book starts with the basics of wireless networks, progressing toward a detailed explanation of cellular networks, fixed wireless networks, and mobile ad hoc networks. Further, wireless personal area networks and wireless sensor networks are discussed in some detail. Also, chapters on IP multimedia services, fundamentals of 5G networks, and the Internet of Things are included for completeness.

The author's presentation style is excellent. She strikes a balance between coverage of topics and depth of presentation. I wholeheartedly congratulate Dr. Mamatha Balachandra for the conception and execution of the book on wireless networks with such coverage, clarity, and presentation style. This book is a very timely and comprehensive contribution to wireless network research literature.

G. Rama Murthy
Mahindra University Bahadurpally
Hyderabad-500043, Telangana
India

PREFACE

Wireless networks are growing day by day in almost all parts of human life. People cannot survive without them even for their household work, for example, booking tickets, getting appointments with doctors, paying bills, purchasing items, *etc.*, from anywhere at any point in time. Wireless networks are useful in reducing networking costs in several cases. As and when their usage increases, there exist several challenges to be faced while using wireless technology. This book gives a basic idea about the evolution and growth of wireless technology, starting from very basic wireless technologies such as GSM and GPRS to WLANs, WPAN, WMANs, cellular networks (from 1G to 5G), and the Internet of Things (IoT).

Nowadays, the Internet of Things is one of the very hot technologies across the globe. All types of organizations, government, private, and industry, are involved in the different aspects, such as implementation, business, and research on IoT. Currently, a lot of investments are being made in almost all these organizations in the development of the Internet of Things. The applications of IoT are broadly in areas like business, healthcare, biometric and facial recognition, inventory tracking, and so on. IoT is used most commonly in smart cities, smart health, smart agriculture, supply chain control, forest fire detection, air pollution detection, *etc.*

The Introduction section of Chapter 1 gives the basics of wireless networks, followed by the evolution of wireless networks, the next wireless network challenges, and various types of wireless networks. Chapter 2 presents generations of cellular networks, *i.e.*, 1G, 2G, 3G, and 4G, in terms of their working, categories, and applications. An overview of WLAN in terms of infrastructure and WLAN technology based on the IEEE 802.11 standard is introduced in Chapter 3. Chapter 4 provides mobile ad hoc network (MANET) challenges, protocols, and various routing algorithms in MANETs. An overview of WPAN in terms of various technologies used, such as ZigBee, Bluetooth, WSN, WISN, *etc.*, is given in Chapter 5. Chapter 6 presents the overview of WSN, categories of WSN, WSN architecture, and WSN coverage and connectivity. An overview of IMS (IP Multimedia Subsystem), the technology that merged with the cellular world, is provided in terms of its architecture, applications, and developing services within the IMS in Chapter 7. An overview of 5G technology in terms of its characteristics, working, and Massive MIMO technology is discussed in Chapter 8. Chapter 9 gives the basics of IoT, IoT connectivity, and IoT use cases, along with the working of sample use cases and important protocols for establishing the connectivity between the IoT devices and the Internet.

Mamatha Balachandra & Balachandra Muniyal
School of Computer Engineering
Manipal Institute of Technology
Manipal Academy of Higher Education
Udupi, Karnataka, India

CHAPTER 1

Introduction to Wireless Networks

Abstract: Wireless Network refers to computer networks without wired connections wherein nodes communicate with each other using radio frequency connections. One of the key benefits of wireless networks is that they can be easily deployed anytime and anywhere for applications such as homes, industry automation, military, agriculture, business, *etc*. This chapter discusses the basics of wireless networks, followed by wireless network evolution, wireless network challenges, the type of wireless network, and how wireless networks are integrated with the Internet of Things (IoT).

Keywords: Challenges, Evolution, IoT, Radio, Wireless networks.

INTRODUCTION

A computer network is a collection of two or more connected computers. Through these networks, people can share data as well as hardware resources and communicate with each other. Computer networks are broadly categorized under two headings: Wired and Wireless networks.

The basic component required for building networks is at least two computers. When we say computer, it need not be just a computer; instead, it can be even a small computing device. We can also have wireless Ad hoc networks, where each computing device is a small microcontroller, sensor, or other device. The other requirement is that there should be a Network Interface Card (NIC) in each computer, a connection medium, which can be a wireless medium, and a network operating system software that controls all of these.

In a wired scenario, a hub or switch is used to connect computers in the network. Here, the responsibility of the hub is to forward data packets from one computer to another. In wireless networks, Mobile Switching Centers act like central hubs. Hubs forward any data packet from one workstation to another [1].

We can use hubs to connect to access, wherein we can connect to LANs. Another important networking component is the router. The responsibility of the router is to route the packet from the source node to the destination node, which also maintains a routing table to determine the next hop. The entire data is divided into packets, which travel in the most efficient paths. It is the responsibility of the router to transmit the packet. Routers are also used to connect any network in a wide area network.

The next device in a wireless network is the access point, which performs the operations like the hub. The access point avoids a wired connection. Some access points have roaming functionality. Access points can connect a wired network to a wireless network so that access points help get service from a wired network to a wireless network. Access points help extend or add more devices to the network. They act like a bridge between wired Ethernet or fast Ethernet Networks. They are very useful in adding more computers to the lab. A sample example wireless network is shown in Fig. (**1**).

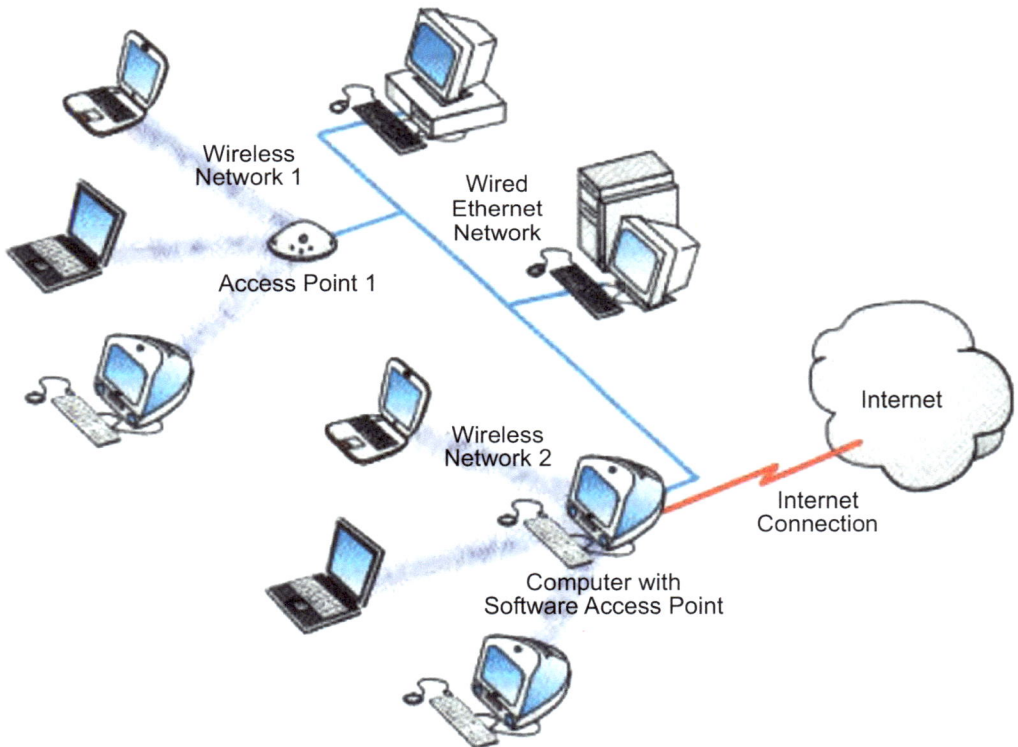

Fig. (1). Sample Wireless Network.

Wireless LAN (WLAN) is an alternative to wired LAN. Using RF technology, users of WLAN can access information over the air without the need to establish a physical connection. By using WLAN, anybody can access shared information without plugging in and looking for a place to plug in. It is a huge advantage of WLAN.

Wireless networks are growing day by day in almost all parts of human life. People cannot survive without them, even for their household work, for example, booking tickets, getting appointments with doctors, paying bills, purchasing items, *etc.*, from anywhere at any point in time.

One of the reasons for using wireless networks in our day-to-day real-life applications is due to their cost-effectiveness. As and when their usage increases, there exist several challenges to be faced while using wireless technology.

EVOLUTION OF WIRELESS NETWORKS

In the first-generation wireless technology, analog ARMs were used. These are cordless telephones (CT) with different standards across the globe. CT1, CT2, and CT3 were the various cordless telephone standards. The specialty of the 1G network is that they were analog and used frequency division multiplexing with limited roaming. There was no real standard across the globe. The MSC was very big. The progress of wireless networks was happening in three geographical regions, which were Europe, the US, and Japan.

In the second-generation GSM technology, GSM 800 and GSM 900 were developed. The specialty of 2G is it uses digital and Time Division Multiplexing Access based primarily on more roaming with better performance and smart billing. Other features are mobile-to-mobile calls, power-controlled Dynamic channel allocation, mobile-assisted handoff, *etc*. This is more robust compared to 1G systems. GSM is one of the most successful wireless technologies that is used even now across the world. Japan came up with PDC in the second generation. The US went towards digital arms, then IS 54, PCS900, and CDMA-based IS95. Europe moved towards GSM 900. GPRS and Edge are moving towards the 3G system.

In 3G, the basic philosophy is one world standard. Cordless and wireless technology converged. Wireless phones are connected to IP, *i.e.*, we can make VOIP calls through cellular phones. The same device acts like a cordless phone inside a home or a cellular phone outside the home, and if we are near an access point, we can make VOIP. This is how the 3G network has emerged. 3G has a combination of various features with better voice quality and video quality. 3G is not only about higher speed but also about a greater number of services with better Quality of Service (QoS) and mobility.

WIRELESS NETWORK CHALLENGES

Power Consumption

The first and most important challenge is to consume less power. The reason for less power consumption is important for 2 things: The first reason to consume less power is to have a battery that lasts for a long time. For example, sending a Multimedia Messaging Service (MMS) may consume more power, but a lot of research is being conducted on how to utilize the battery more efficiently. To avoid this, the hardware is designed in such a way that it is less power-hungry. The second reason is to have certain signal processing tools to ensure that it only extends power when required.

Efficient Spectrum Usage

As we know, the spectrum is scarce in wireless communication. If we have finite bandwidth requirements, there are pre-decided capacity relations that tell us how much we can go, provided the signal-to-power ratio is so much. How can we use it better? Why do we have only one transmitter/receiver antenna? Why do not we have multiple input and multiple output systems? The solution is making use of multiple input, multiple output (MIMO) technology.

Integrated Customer Services

Assume that we have data, voice, and multimedia with low power and low bandwidth requirements. Suppose there is a smaller share of bandwidth with a greater number of users sharing bandwidth. We need to see the technique to do so. For example, when we are talking on the phone, the delay should not be greater than a certain amount. While sending VOIP, it goes through a large wireless network where the overall delay should not be so much. We need to take care of packet loss, data rate, and bit error rate. The data rate is very important when streaming videos. A bursty traffic needs to be talked about differently.

Network Support for user Mobility

We must provide the user with enough mobility. Suppose the person is traveling and using a mobile phone; then there will be mobility. Then, a handover may happen, *i.e.*, one base station must hand over the call to another base station.

QoS (Quality of Service)

The performance of the wireless network is measured in terms of QoS parameters such as delay, throughput, jitter, packet loss, *etc*. QoS in the wireless network is based on various factors such as routing, mobility, transmission medium, noise, and so forth. QoS requirements are different for different applications. To accept the working of any application, it is desirable to meet the required QoS parameters; otherwise, the application will not be sustained.

Connectivity and Coverage

Today, if a new internet service provider or new mobile user comes in, we need to give enough coverage, *i.e.*, 99%. So, coverage is a big issue.

Fading

Fading in wireless communication is largely due to multipath propagation, where signals travel from the transmitter to the receiver through multiple paths. At the receiver end, the shifted rays get superimposed. How does the antenna pick up the signal when more than one radiation comes at the same time from a different transmitter? It superimposes.There is a risk that the signal received may be completely different from what was originally transmitted. This makes it one of the most difficult challenges to address in wireless communication.

Security

Security is also another big issue. Anybody can listen to what you are speaking by putting an antenna. Today, most mobile phones have built-in security. But for every lock, the computer makes a key. This is ever-evolving in the research area.

ELECTROMAGNETIC SPECTRUM

Electromagnetic waves are periodic oscillations that carry energy from one location to another. These waves do not require a medium, and they can travel through space. The shorter the wavelength of the wave, the more energy it carries. There seems to be no upper and lower limit on the wavelength of the electromagnetic wave. The name for all these possible wavelengths put together is the electromagnetic spectrum. The wave's frequency is determined by the speed of the electron. A sample electromagnetic wave with appropriate frequency and amplitude is shown in Fig. (**2**).

The electromagnetic spectrum is licensed bands, and the government generates a lot of money out of it. There is a Telephone Regulatory Authority of India (TRAI) that works on these issues. There exist several frequency bands in the electromagnetic spectrum. Different frequencies get attenuated in air differently. For wireless communication, air is the channel. Frequency (FM) radio works at 88MHz, GSM phones work at 900GHz, and Bluetooth and Wi-Fi work at 2.4 GHz, which is the favorite band of industrial, scientific, and medical radio (ISM). Wireless communication between large distances requires more power. When we increase power, it requires more money. Radiation is another aspect. The mobile phone that we are using must comply with a certain maximum radiated power. If we simply increase the power of radiation, nearby people get affected. Lower-frequency rays also travel larger distances. Other aspects are rain, dust, and fog. The electromagnetic wave is affected by these particles. Fig. (**3**) shows the electromagnetic spectrum with different frequency bands.

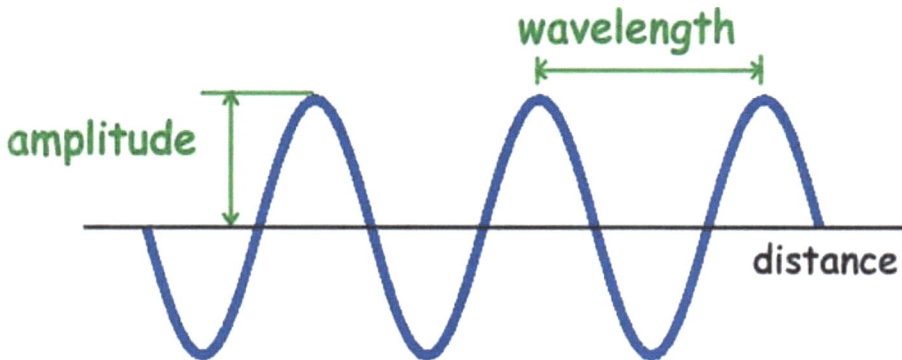

Fig. (2). Electromagnetic wave [2].

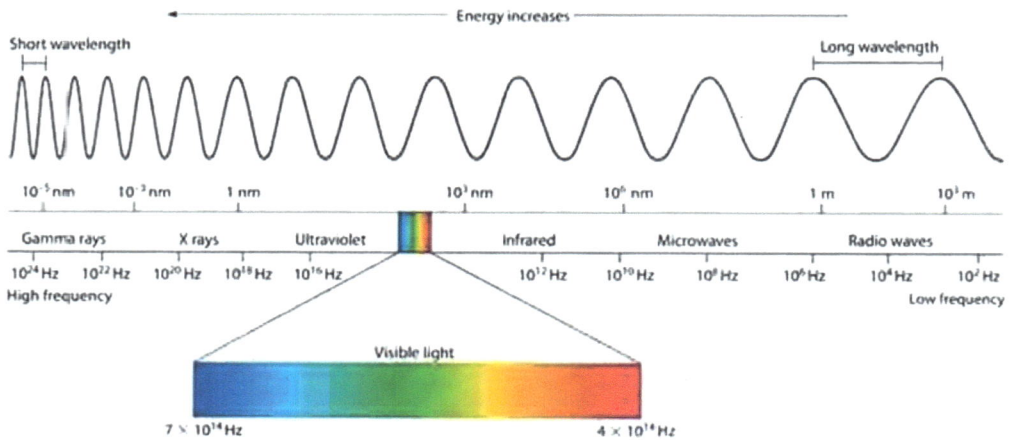

Fig. (3). Electromagnetic spectrum with different frequency bands [3].

WIRELESS TRANSMISSION AND FREQUENCY SPECTRUM

In wired transmission, there is no problem of interference. However, in the case of wireless transmission, there is more interference due to the transmission medium, and the use of radio spectrum for the transmission is regulated. One of the major design issues concerning wireless transmission is multiplexing because the wireless medium is always shared. So, here the requirement is to ensure low interference between different senders by multiplexing schemes.

Fig. (**4**) roughly shows the frequency spectrum that can be used for data transmission [4].

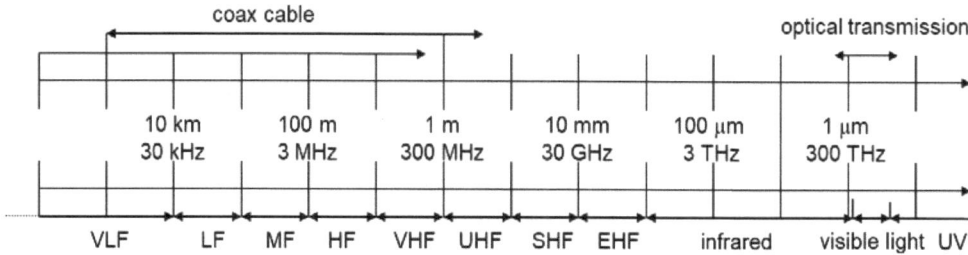

Fig. (4). Frequency spectrum for data transmission.

As shown in Fig. (**4**), radio transmission usually starts at a very low frequency (VLF) range, which means at several kHz. Understanding the radio spectrum and the different wavelengths and frequencies is key to understanding the properties of the spectrum. Differing wavelengths and frequencies mean that signals have different properties and can be used in different ways: long-distance radio communication, point-to-point communication, satellite communications, and many more.

Names like LF, MF, HF, VHF, UHF, SHF, *etc.*, represent the portions of the radio frequency spectrum. The ITU (International Telecommunication Union) is a global organization regulating the usage of the frequency spectrum. Originally, there were only 9 bands, as per ITU. But, as the extent of usage and future usage of the radio spectrum has increased, there are now 12 bands. As shown in Fig. (**4**), VLF (Low Frequency) operates at 3 to 30kHz with wavelengths up to 10-kilometers. LF (Low Frequency) operates at 30 to 300 kHz with wavelengths up to 1 kilometer. MF (Medium Frequency) operates at 300 to 3000kHz with wavelengths up to 100 meters. HF (High Frequency) operates at 3 to 30MHz with wavelengths up to 10 meters. VHF (Very High Frequency) operates at 30 to 300MHz with wavelengths up to 1 meter. UHF (Ultra High Frequency) operates at 300 to 3000MHz with wavelengths up to 10 centimeters. SHF (Super High Frequency) operates at 3 to 30GHz with wavelengths up to 1 centimeter. EHF (Extremely High Frequency) operates at 30 to 300GHz with wavelengths up to 1 millimeter.

The International Telecommunications Union (ITU), located in Geneva, is responsible for worldwide coordination of telecommunication activities (wired and wireless). All these frequencies, which are discussed here, are regulated to avoid interference during the transmission.

Some ranges of frequencies used for mobile phones and wireless LANs are discussed here. These ranges are different with respect to different countries. For example, in Europe, GSM mobile phone operates in the following ranges of frequencies: 890–915, 935–960, 1710–1785, and 1805–1880; whereas in the US, GSM mobile phone operates in frequency ranges of1850–1910 and 1930–1990.

One of the very popular wireless networks is GSM. As per the survey, GSM is available in over 220 countries, and it is used by more than 5 billion people (GSM World, 2018). GSM has evolved into new-generation mobile networks such as 3G, 4G, and 5G.

Another popular short-range wireless network, WLAN standards, is of special interest for wireless, mobile computer communication, which can be used on a campus or in buildings. One of the attractive benefits of WLAN is that it provides a license-free ISM band for industry-developed products at the frequency range of 2.4 GHZ, which is available across the globe.

MODULATION TECHNIQUES

Let us first understand the concept of modulation. Modulation is a process of varying one or more properties of a periodic waveform called a carrier signal with the modulating signal that typically contains the information to be transmitted. In telecommunications, modulation is a process of conveying a message signal, for example, a digital bitstream or analog audio signal, inside another signal that can physically be transmitted. Modulation is a sign waveform that transforms a baseband message signal into a passband signal. To understand why modulation is required, we can consider an example of a letter and an envelope. Here, the input message signal represents the letter that we write. In this example, without writing a proper address on the envelope, the letter cannot be sent to the intended recipient. Hence, we use an envelope to write the proper recipient address on it and then insert the letter in that envelope and seal it so that the letter is received by the intended recipient. In the same way, we modulate the signal(envelope) properly in such a way that the message is sent to the intended recipient only. The carrier signal (the postman) is a sinusoidal wave that makes it possible for us to send the signal through the channel. A modulator is a device that performs the modulation.

With the wireless network, the data to be communicated can be either analog or digital. To send this data over a wireless channel, it has to be converted into electromagnetic waves. This phenomenon, which is used to perform the conversion of analog or digital data into electromagnetic waves, is called the modulation technique. This technique works by allotting a carrier wave containing the frequency of the wireless channel, which is a property of a radio wave. Modulation techniques are broadly classified under two headings: Analog and digital [5].

Analog Modulation Techniques

Analog modulation aims to transmit an analog baseband or low pass signal (for example, an audio signal or TV signal). There are 2 types of analog modulation techniques. They are Frequency modulation and Amplitude modulation. An Amplitude modulation technique works by varying the amplitude of the carrier wave, whereas a Frequency modulation technique works by varying the frequency of the carrier wave.

Amplitude Modulation

Modulation is a process of changing the characteristics of a carrier signal with a message signal. The message signal modulates the carrier signal. The modulated carrier signal is sent to the receiver. Amplitude modulation changes the amplitude of the carrier wave to convey information. Since the amplitude of the carrier wave is changed by the intensity of the signal, the process is called amplitude modulation. However, the frequency and phase of the carrier wave do not change.

Fig. (**5**) shows the sample carrier wave, analog signal, and the resultant amplitude-modulated signal.

Frequency Modulation

In frequency modulation, instead of altering the amplitude of the carrier wave, the frequency of the carrier wave is altered. Frequency modulation is more advantageous compared to the amplitude modulation technique as there is no interference problem with frequency modulation as the background noise is less resistant to noise than amplitude modulation since, most of the time, noise affects the amplitude of the signal more than the frequency. Most music radio stations prefer FM over AM to transmit information (mostly songs) to their listeners due to the much better quality of transmission. Fig. (**6**) shows the sample carrier wave, analog signal, and the resultant frequency-modulated signal.

Radio and television broadcasts and satellite radio typically use AM or FM. Most two-way radios use FM.

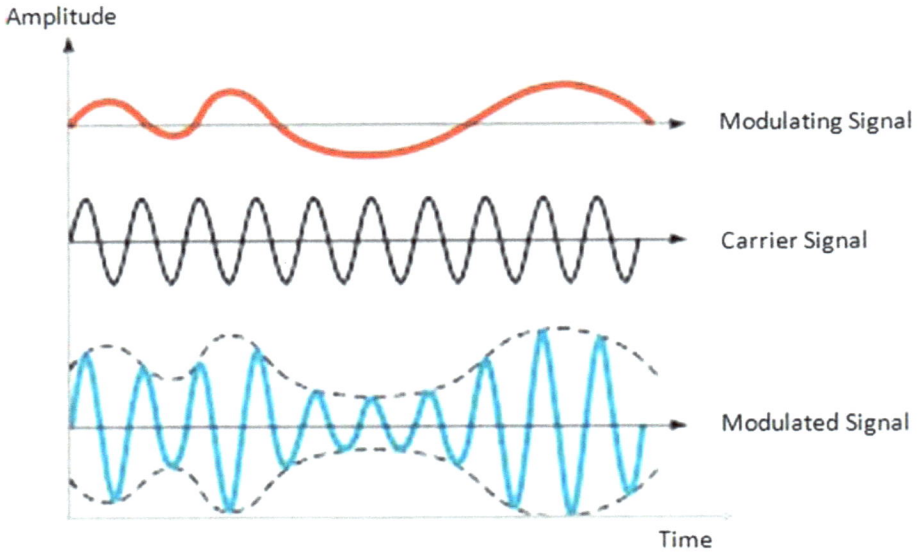

Fig. (5). Sample Amplitude modulation.

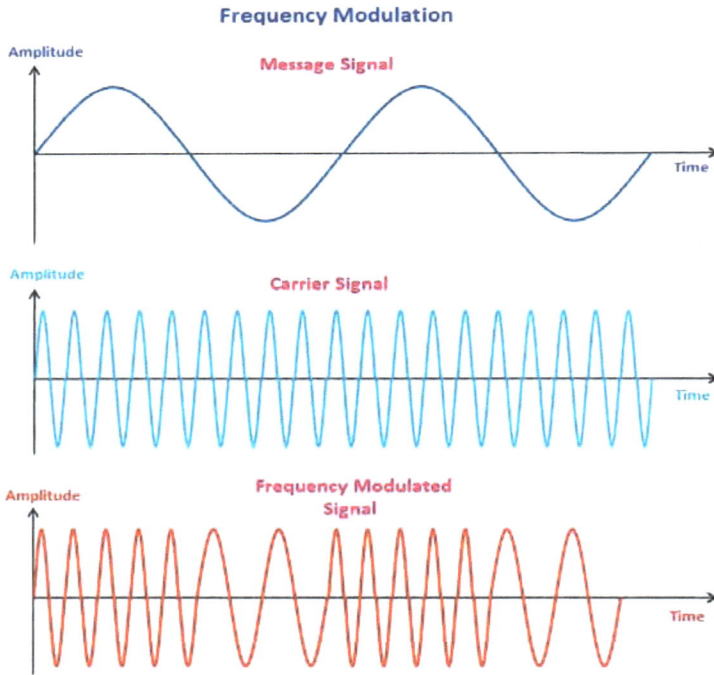

Fig. (6). Sample Frequency Modulation [6].

Digital Modulation Techniques

Digital modulation provides more information capacity, high data security, and quicker system availability with a high quality of communication. It works by converting the bit stream (digital data) to a suitable continuous waveform. Digital modulation also alters the property of carrier waves, as in the case of analog modulation. Amplitude Shift Keying, Frequency Shift Keying, and Phase Shift Keying are the three different classifications of digital modulation techniques.

SPECTRUM ALLOCATION TECHNIQUES

As many users use the same channel at the same time and the capacity of the spectrum is limited, sharing is required to increase usage by allowing different users to make use of the available bandwidth at the same time. A cellular system divides any given large geographic location into cells where a mobile unit in each cell can move from one cell to another to communicate with each other and also with the base station. The advantage of this design is to improve the channel capacity by having a sufficient level of QoS in terms of bandwidth. The three different ways of accessing the wireless channel are Time-division multiple-access (TDMA), Frequency-division multiple access (FDMA), and code-division multiple-access (CDMA) [6].

Frequency Division Multiple Access (FDMA)

In FDMA, the spectrum is divided into sub bands that are used by one or more users, as shown in Fig. (7). Each user is provided a dedicated channel. For each user pair of channels are allocated (uplink and downlink). The Uplink channel operates with less frequency than the downlink channel. FDMA is used in 1G cellular systems.

The advantages of FDMA are that no dynamic coordination is necessary, and it also works for analog signals. There are several disadvantages of FDMA, which include bandwidth wastage, inflexibility, uneven distribution of the traffic, and the requirement of guard spaces to get rid of adjacent channel interference.

Time Division Multiple Access (TDMA)

In TDMA, a channel gets the whole spectrum for a certain amount of time, as shown in Fig. (8). TDMA is one of the important technologies of choice for many 2G cellular systems, such as GSM, IS-54, *etc.* It divides the entire band into several time slots called TDMA frames. In this technique, one or more slots for the transmission of traffic are assigned to each active node. Here, each node gets the notification regarding the specific slot number, and also, they know how much they need to wait within the TDMA frame. In TDMA, Uplink or Downlink channels can occur either in Frequency Division Duplexing (FDD)-TDMA or in Time Division Duplexing (TDD)-TDMA. Among these two, the latter (TDD-TDMA) has more advantages while taking into account uplink to downlink bandwidth tracking for supporting asymmetric traffic patterns. TDMA is essentially half-duplex, *i.e.*, among a pair of communicating nodes, only one node can be transmitted. There are chances that the node misses its turn in case the slot duration is very small because the nodes are far from each other.

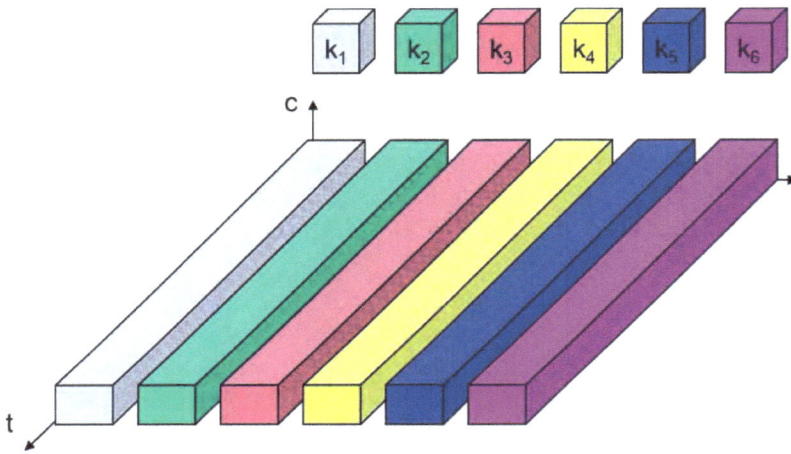

Fig. (7). Sample FDMA.

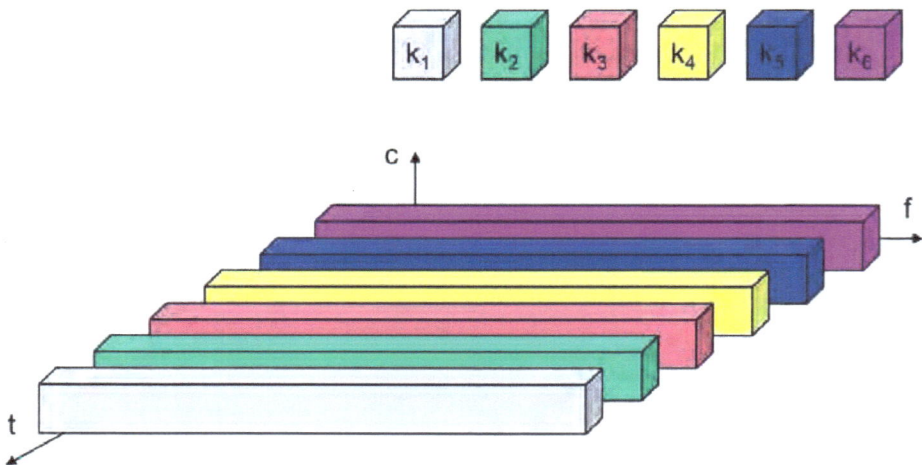

Fig. (8). Sample TDMA.

The advantages of TDMA are that there is only one carrier in the medium at any time, and also throughput is high even if there are many users. One of the major disadvantages of TDMA is that precise synchronization is necessary.

A combination of both FDMA and TDMA can be used wherein the channel gets a certain frequency band for a certain amount of time, as shown in Fig. (**9**). The benefit of this approach is protection against frequency, protection against message tapping, selective interference, and data transmission at higher rates with precise coordination.

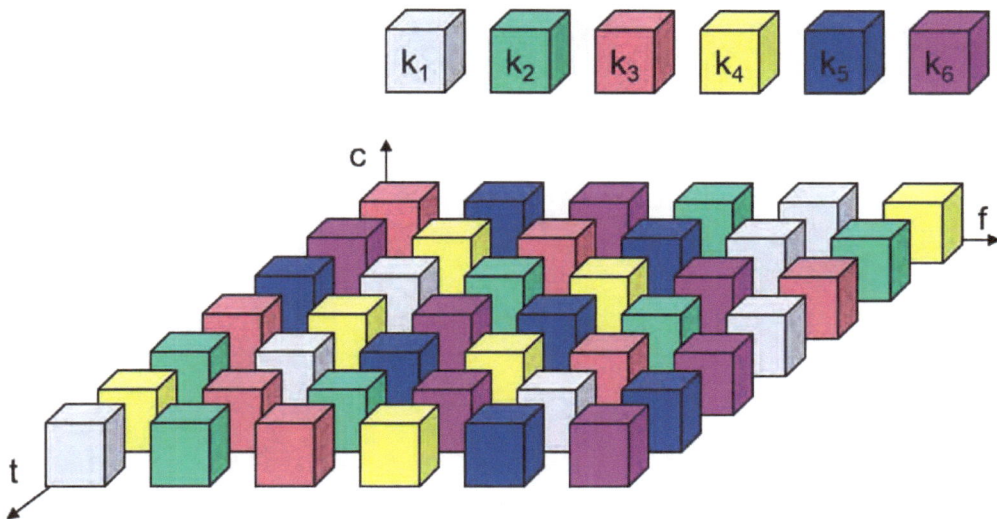

Fig. (9). Sample FDMA/TDMA.

Code Division Multiple Access (CDMA)

Sample CDMA is shown in Fig. (**10**). One of the characteristics of CDMA is that it keeps all nodes in the same bandwidth at the same time instead of sharing the available bandwidth either in terms of frequency or time. Here, multiple users' transmission is separated with the help of an n-bit unique code that is assigned to each node. N-bit chip code is assigned to all nodes in the network, and the value of n is known as the chip rate. The codes assigned are orthogonal to each other, *i.e.*, the normalized inner product of the vector representation of any pair of codes is zero. In order to perform decoding, the receiver must also know the codes of each user [7].

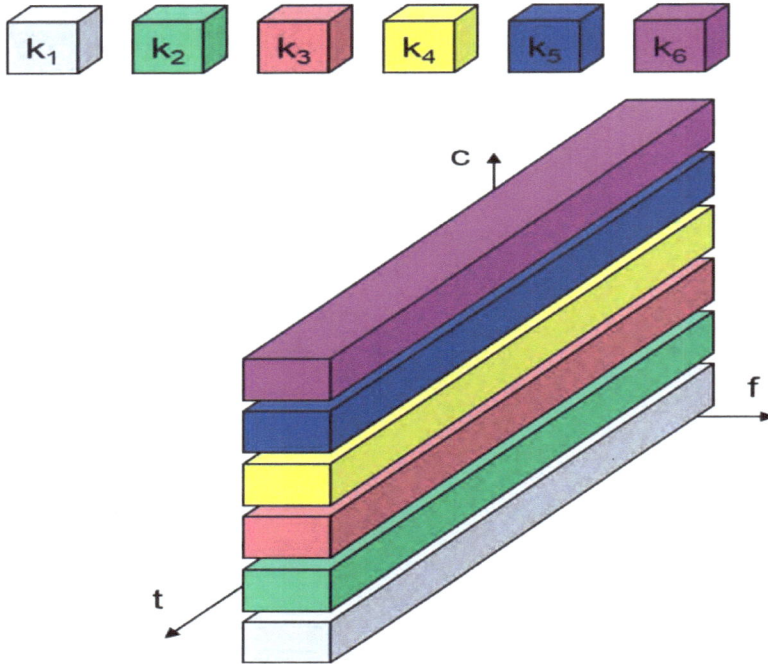

Fig. (10). Sample CDMA.

Some of the advantages of CDMA are that it does not require coordination and synchronization, provides good protection against interference, and is bandwidth efficient. The disadvantages of CDMA are lower user data rates and more complex signal regeneration.

TDMA can be combined with CDMA for better usage. The advantages of using TDMA/CDMA in cellular systems are listed below:

  i. Simple System
 ii. Flexibility of mixed voice/data communication.
iii. Costs are reduced.
 iv. Reduced RF power.
  v. Natural integration with digital wireless network.

CELLULAR CONCEPT

Fig. (**11**) shows the typical cellular network.

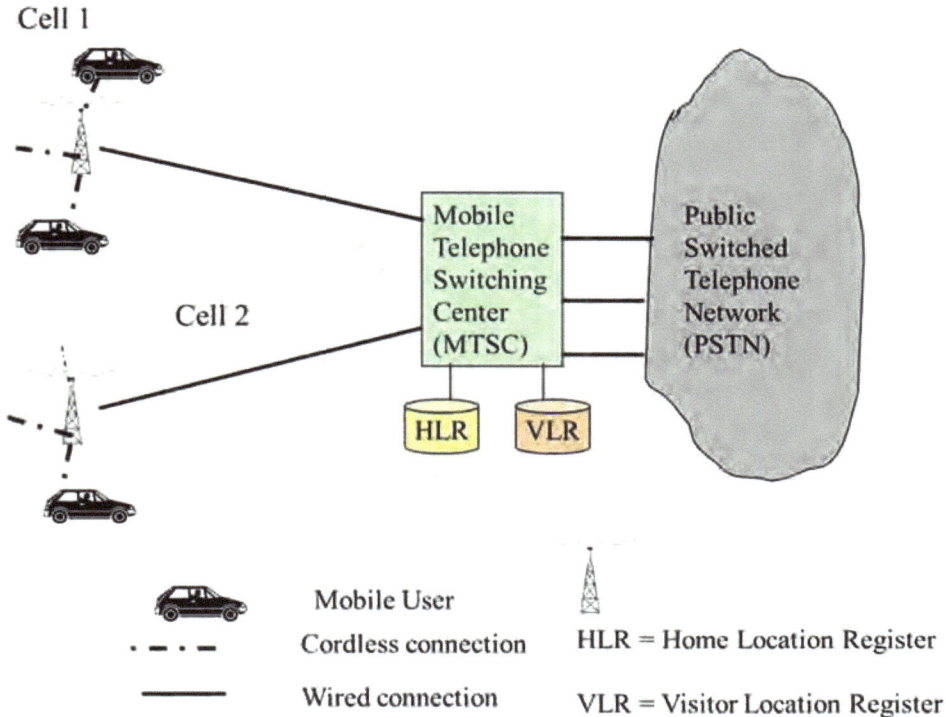

Fig. (11). A typical Cellular Network.

At any time, the mobile station (MS) is in one cell and is under the control of a Base Station(BS). When an MS leaves a cell, BS notices a weak signal. The BS asks the surrounding BSs whether they are getting a stronger signal. Then, the BS transfers its ownership to the one with the strongest signal. MTSC assigns a new channel to MS and notifies MS of the new boss. The purpose of the wireless network is to have access to the fixed network (PSTN).

Frequency Reuse

The concept of frequency reuse is based on assigning to each cell a group of radio channels used within a small geographic area.

- Cells are assigned a group of channels that is completely different from neighboring cells.
- The coverage area of cells is called the footprint and is limited by a boundary so that the same group of channels can be used in cells that are far apart.

Here, cells with the same number have the same set of frequencies, as shown in Fig. (**12a, b**) shows Frequency Reuse using 7 frequency allocations. Each cell is generally 4 to 8 miles in diameter, with a lower limit of around 2 miles.

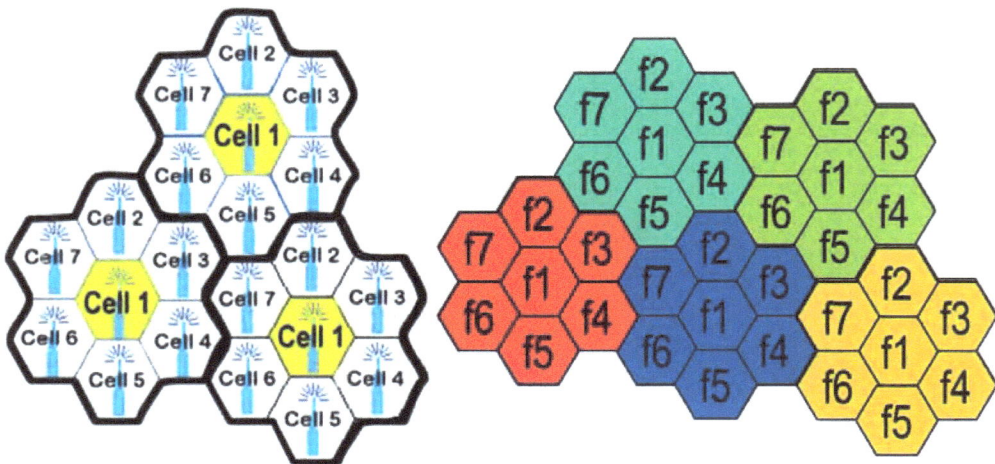

Fig. (12). (**a**) Frequency reuse (**b**) Frequency reuse using frequency.

Allocations

Even though it might seem natural to choose a circle to represent the coverage area of the base station, adjacent circles cannot be overlaid on a map without leaving gaps or creating overlapping regions. Thus, when considering geometric shapes that cover the entire region without overlap and with equal area, there are 3 choices: equilateral triangle, square, and hexagon. Among these, the hexagonal cell shape is preferred over the square and the triangle shapes because:

- the area occupied by the hexagonal cell shape is larger than the square and the triangle; thus, to cover a certain geographical region, fewer cells will be used.
- a hexagonal cell shape closely approximates the circular radiation pattern (used by today's Omnidirectional antennas) of the base station (*i.e.*, transmitter). Circular cell shapes are not used because of the gaps they leave in between them if implemented.

*The frequency reuse facto*r of the cellular system is given by 1/N since each cell within a cluster is only assigned 1/N of the total available channels.

Let 'S' be the total available channels. 'N' is the adjacent cells (called a cluster) that share 'S' channels.

Each cell gets k channels:

$S = k N$

Suppose the system has 'M' clusters; then the capacity of the system is:

$C = MkN = MS$

Types of Wireless Networks

Based on the range of communication, usage, and communication protocols used, wireless networks are classified into four categories, as shown in Table **1**.

Table 1. Classification of wireless networks.

Type of Network	Area of Coverage	Applications	Communication Protocols used
Wireless Personal area network (WPAN)	Connecting Tablets, Laptops, and Smartphones within 10 meters	Used to transmit small files such as music, appointments, *etc*.	Bluetooth, Infrared, Near Field Communication (NFC), IEEE 802.15
Wireless Local area network (WLAN)	Connecting Computers, Printers, and Switches within a building or campus	Use high-frequency radio waves instead of cables for connecting the devices within the building to connect devices for sharing resources.	IEEE 802.11 (Wi-Fi)
Wireless Metropolitan Area Network (WMAN)	To connect several buildings within a city	Wireless inter-network connectivity within various departments of an organization with low-cost	IEEE 802.16 (WiMAX)
Wireless Wide Area Network (WWAN)	Worldwide	Wide range of applications connectivity through cell phones, satellites, IoTs, WSN	4G (LTE), 5G

WPANS (IEEE 802.15) allows the connectivity of personal devices within an area of about a few feet. WLANs (IEEE 802.11) allow users in proximity, such as within a library or University, to form a network or gain access to the internet. WMANS (IEEE 802.16) allows for communication within a few meters in a metropolitan area, such as different buildings in a city, which allows the connection of different networks *via* fiber or copper cabling. Finally, WWAN (4G: LTE, 5G) is a wireless area network that can cover large geographical areas.

Integration of Wireless Networks with IoT (Internet of Things)

Wi-Fi is a standard for Wireless Fidelity that refers to the IEEE 802.11 standard for wireless local networks or WLANs, which connect computers to the Internet and the wired networks. Wi-Fi uses radio technology to transmit and receive data at high speed. The important features of Wi-Fi such as its simplicity, ubiquity, and user-friendliness, provide connectivity standards for IoT devices and afford to embed them in IoT. So, most of the IoT devices today are embedded with Wi-Fi chips. Thus, Wi-Fi technology is used to connect IoT devices to the Internet.

CONCLUDING REMARKS

This chapter gives the basics of wireless networks, starting from how wireless communication evolved and what challenges need to be faced in this network compared to wired counterparts. Various modulation techniques, such as FDMA, TDMA, and CDMA, are also explained.

EXERCISES

1. What do you mean by wireless network? How is it different from the fixed network?
2. List and explain the challenges of wireless networks.
3. Differentiate between FDMA and TDMA.
4. List the advantages and disadvantages of TDMA.
5. Explain the working of CDMA.
6. Four channels are multiplexed using TDM. If each channel sends 100 bytes /s and we multiplex 1 byte per channel, show the frame traveling on the link, the size of the frame, the duration of a frame, the frame rate, and the bit rate for the link.
7. Four channels, two with a bit rate of 200 kbps and two with a bit rate of 150 kbps, are to be multiplexed using multiple slots TDM with no synchronization bits. Answer the following questions:
   a. What is the size of a frame in bits?
   b. What is the frame rate?
   c. What is the duration of a frame?
   d. What is the data rate?
8. If a total of 33 MHz of bandwidth is allocated to a particular FDD cellular telephone system, which uses two 25 KHz simplex channels to provide full duplex voice and control channels. Compute the number of channels available per cell if a system uses (a) 4-cell reuses, (b) 7-cell reuses, and (c) 12-cell reuses.
9. Why is a hexagonal cell shape perfect over square or triangular cell shapes in cellular architecture?
10. Using the CDMA technique, If sender0 has code $(1, -1)$ and data $(1, 0, 1, 1)$, and Sender1 has code $(1, 1)$ and data $(0, 0, 1, 1)$, and both senders transmit simultaneously, then describe the coding steps.

Through the integration of Wi-Fi and IoT, we can control home appliances such as light bulbs, AC, or fans using our smartphone, and we can monitor the room temperature and humidity of our home remotely from anywhere in the world. For example, if you are in the USA, you can remotely monitor the room temperature, humidity, *etc.*, of your hometown in India. Fig. (**13**) shows Wi-Fi-based IoT for home automation.

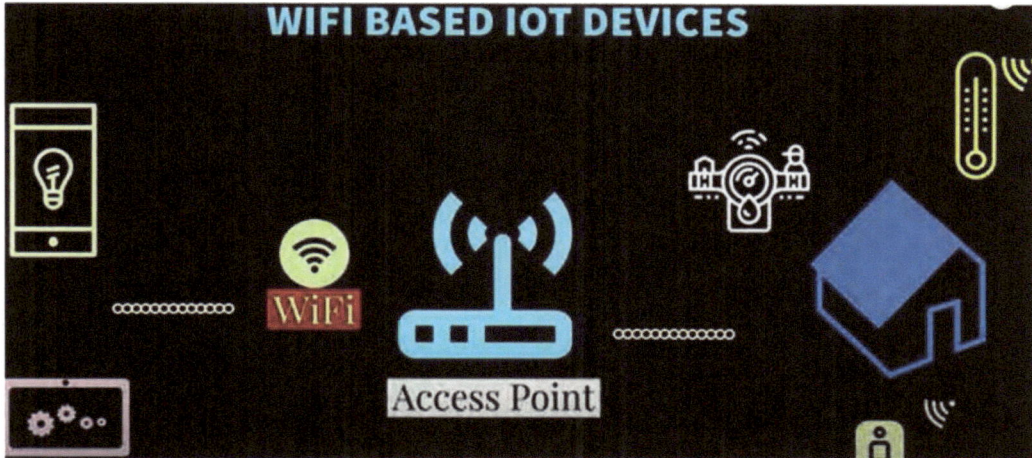

Fig. (13). Wi-Fi-based IoT for home automation.

REFERENCES

[1]   K. Pahlavan, A.H. Levesque, "Wireless Information Networks", *john wiley & sons, inc., publication,* 2005.

[2]   Available from: https://www.ducksters.com/science/physics/properties_of_waves.php

[3]   Available   from: https://www.quora.com/Does-light-only-exist-until-the-far-infra-red-and-far-ultraviolet-bands-Are-there-other-spectra

[4]   W. Stallings, "Wireless communications and networks", *Pearson Prentice Hall® is a trademark of Pearson Education, Inc,* 2005.

[5]   Available from: https://archive.nptel.ac.in/courses/117/102/117102062/

[6]   Available from: https://www.physics-and-radio-electronics.com/blog/frequency-modulation/

[7]   Available from: https://ebin.pub/wireless-networks-9780470845295-0470845295.html

CHAPTER 2

Cellular Networks

Abstract: A cellular network refers to a mobile network wherein nodes distributed across long distances communicate with each other using radio frequency connections. Cellular wireless networks divide large geographic areas into sections or cells, each served by at least one transceiver. In this chapter, various generations of cellular networks, 1G, 2G, 3G, and 4G, in terms of their working, categories, and applications are discussed. Also, technologies that are used, especially in 3G and 4G cellular networks such as WCDMA and OFDM, are explained.

Keywords: 1G, 2G, 3G, 4G, CDMA, GPRS, GSM, OFDM, UMTS, WCDMA.

INTRODUCTION

Today, a cellular network is a common man's technology. The wireless network is not equal to the cellular network, but it is much bigger. Cellular technology happens to be the most dominant technology. Cellular technology is much more than WPAN (Wireless Personal Area Network) or WLAN (Wireless Local Area Network). A cellular network is a WWAN (Wireless Wide Area Network) that covers large geographical areas, which is much bigger than WPAN and WLAN.

The base stations are every 500 meters to cover the wireless range. Unfortunately, the range is good, but the interference is bad, and we need to have the proper balance between interference and the range.

Cellular technology is a licensed technology, which means we cannot transmit through cellular networks without licensed bands. Before the smartphones that we are using now, there were several versions of phones such as Motorola Micro Tac (1986), Nokia 101 (1992), Motorola StarTAC(1996), Blackberry 5810(2002), Apple Phone (2007), iPhone (2012), *etc.* This is the evolution that happened in terms of handsets. But in terms of functionality, we can categorize them into 1G, 2G, 3G, 4G, 5G, and so on. Each cellular network generation is the improved version of the previous generation in terms of data rate, access technology, bandwidth, range of coverage, *etc.*

1G: ANALOG CELLULAR SYSTEM

In 1946, the first telephone system, which is known as MTS (Mobile Telephone System) was introduced. They had several disadvantages, which are mentioned below:

a. Transceivers were very huge, and vehicles were used to carry them.
b. Inefficient usage of the Spectrum.
c. Manual call switching.

The major difference between MTS and 1G cellular systems was that 1G made use of the cellular concept. The cellular concept greatly improves spectrum usage. The 1G cellular phone was analog, *i.e.*, it made use of analog signaling for communicating. Due to this, the following problems arose:

i. Encryption is not possible: There is no encryption of the traffic in a 1G system. So, voice calls through such networks are susceptible to interception, causing them to be vulnerable to eavesdropping. Also, there is a possibility of revealing user identification numbers, thus placing illegal calls by listening to the channels.
ii. Inferior call quality: Analog signaling for communication results in inferior call quality as it is easily degraded by interferences.
iii. Spectrum inefficiency: Since each Radio Frequency (RF) carrier is dedicated to a single user in the case of analog signaling, irrespective of whether the user is active or not, it results in inefficient spectrum utilization.

Analog systems have been deployed worldwide during the first generation of cellular systems. In the United States, the Analog Mobile Telephone System (AMTS) was developed in 1982, offering voice transmission. Advanced Mobile Phone System (AMPS) was developed during the early 1980s by Bell Laboratories. It was designed to provide mobile telephone traffic services *via* the number of 30KHz channels between base stations and mobile stations of each call. All these 30KHz channels were used to carry voice traffic [1].

Advanced Mobile Phone System

During the 1980s, the first allocation of bandwidth for AMPS was made by the Federal Communication Commission (FCC) in order to test systems in the Chicago area. The allocation bandwidth was in the 800MHz part of the spectrum. This is because above 800MHz was a very densely used allocation of frequencies in the bands of AMPS, which caused severe attenuation due to path loss or fading. Also, the 800MHz band was a relatively unused band.

AMPS Channels

AMPS had two sets of channels: A (1 to 333) and B (334 to 666). Channels 313 to 333 and 334 to 354 are the control channels of channels A and B, respectively. Each operator has 21 control channels and 312 voice channels.

Traffic channels are 30KHz analog FM channels to serve the voice traffic. The main traffic channels are the Forward Voice Channel (FVC) and Reverse Voice Channel (RVC), carrying voice traffic from the Base Station (BS) to the Mobile Station (MS) and from MS to BS.

Control channels (CC) carry digital signaling and are used to coordinate medium access of mobile stations. The main control channels are the Forward Control Channel (FCC) and the Reverse Control Channel (RCC).

Supervisory Audio Tone (SAT) is sent on the voice channel to enable MSs and BSs to process information on the quality of the link and to ensure link continuity.

The signaling tone of AMPS is used to send four signals: (i) A *request to send* whose task is to allow the user to enter more data, (ii) an *alert signal,* which is continuously sent until the user of MS answers the call, (iii) a *discount call* sent by MS over RVC, which is to indicate the termination of the call, and (iv) the handoff of the current MS to another BS is done by sending handoff information by MS in response to network request [2].

Network Operations

a. Electronic Serial Number (ESN): A string of 32 bits uniquely identifies AMPS MS. This number is set by the MS manufacturer and is burned into ROM to prevent unauthorized changes of the number. If someone tries to rewrite ESN, MS will become inoperable. The 18-bit Manufacturers code (MFR) of ESN uniquely identifies each manufacturer; another 6 bits remain unused, and the next 8 bits represent the serial number. If more and more MSs are manufactured, then additional serial numbers in combination with the same MFR can be used to identify new sets of MSs.
b. System Identification Number (SID): This is a 15-bit number that indicates the AMPS network. This is transmitted by BS to MS.
c. Mobile Identification Number (MIN): It is a 34-bit string that is derived from 10 digit telephone number (24 bits from local code + 10 bits from global code).

Initialization

Once the AMPS is powered on, the following events will happen:

  i. MS receives system parameters to use one of AMPS (A or B).
 ii. Among the 21 control channels that are scanned by MS, the selection of a control channel is based on its quality. So, when the acceptable quality meets, it gets selected.
iii. A message on the control channel having system parameters is received by MS.
 iv. MS seeks the SID of AMPS to prepare for roaming or not.
  v. MS identifies itself by sending ESN, SID, and MIN *via* RCC.
 vi. AMPS determines whether MS is roaming or not.
vii. BS verifies initial parameters.
viii. MS goes to an idle state.

2G: CELLULAR SYSTEMS

2G cellular system overcomes the deficiencies of the 1G system. The advantages of digital technology over analog technology are given below:

a. Encryption: To provide privacy and security, encryption can be easily performed with digital systems, whereas it is not possible in analog systems. Encrypted signals cannot be interpreted and overheard by unauthorized parties. On the other hand, powerful encryption is not possible in analog systems.
b. Use of error correction: It is possible to apply error correction and error detection techniques to the user traffic in a digital system. This helps in improving the transmission reliability as compared to analog systems. Due to this, there exist several advantages, such as efficient spectrum usage, higher speeds for data, better voice call qualities, *etc*. This is not possible with an analog system.
c. RF carrier can be shared: Unlike analog systems, in digital systems, it is possible to share RF carrier among more than one user, either by using different codes per user or different time slots.
d. Spectrum allocation: In 2G cellular systems, FDMA was the first spectrum allocation technique used. In this system, with N users and a total bandwidth of W, each user can be assigned a bandwidth of W/N.

Digital Advanced Mobile Phone System (DAMPS)

DAMPS maintains the 30KHz channel spacing of AMPS. The DAMPS handset is designed to operate in dual mode. The key difference between DAMPS to AMPS is that DAMS overlays the digital channel over the 30KHz carrier of AMPS. For the same carrier, the individual user channel in DAMPS can support around three times the users that are supported by AMPS.

Each DAMPS mobile station initially accesses the hardware *via* an AMPS analog control channel. Next, the mobile station can send a request. In AMPS, the handoff is handled by BS, whereas in DAMPS, signal strength measurement is done by MS instead of BS.

DAMPS Channels

DAMPS reuses the channels of AMPS. DAMPs also introduced some of its digital channels. The list of channels of DAMPS is given below:

  i. FCC: Same as AMPS.
 ii. FVC: Here, voice traffic is carried from BS to MS in terms of analog traffic or signal.
iii. FDTC: Here, digital traffic is carried from BS to MS.
 iv. RECC: Like AMPS.
  v. RVC: Like AMPS.
 vi. Reverse Digital Traffic Channel (RDTC): Here, digital traffic is carried from MS to BS.

2G: GSM

GSM was founded in Europe during the 1980s. In the early 1980s, Europe was experiencing the growth of analog cellular systems, mainly TACS and NMT. Other cellular systems that are deployed in Europe are RadioCom 2000 in France, RMTS in Italy, and C450 in Germany. However, the main disadvantage of these systems is they are generally not compatible with each other. This is undesirable because mobile equipment operations were limited within boundaries and limited market for each type of equipment [2].

To solve the above problem, in 1992, a research group called Global Special Mobile, which was further renamed GSM (Global System for Mobile Communication), was formed. The proposed system meets the following criteria:

  a. Good subjective speech quality
  b. Low terminal and low service cost
  c. Support for a range of new services
  d. Spectral efficiency
  e. ISDN compatibility

f. International roaming

g. Support for handheld terminals

GSM was deployed in many countries (approximately 110). Overall, four versions of GSM depend on the operating frequency: GSM 900, GSM 1800, GSM 1900, and GSM 450.

GSM ARCHITECTURE AND MOBILITY MANAGEMENT

Fig. (**1**) shows the Layout of the GSM network.

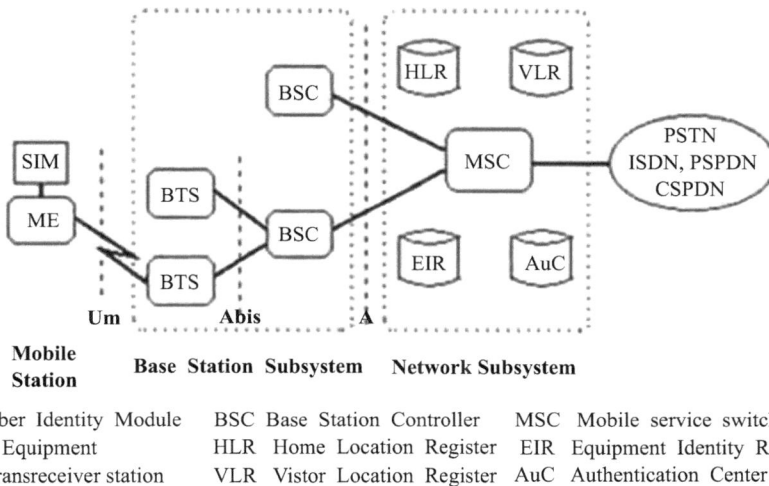

SIM	Subscriber Identity Module	BSC	Base Station Controller	MSC	Mobile service switching center
ME	Mobile Equipment	HLR	Home Location Register	EIR	Equipment Identity Register
BTS	Base Transreceiver station	VLR	Vistor Location Register	AuC	Authentication Center

Fig. (1). Layout of GSM Network Architecture.

Mobile Station (MS)

MS consists of two important modules: the User Equipment, or Mobile Equipment (ME), and the Subscriber Identity Module (SIM) card. Multiple MSs are connected to a single tower. The user can have access to subscriber services irrespective of the specific terminal using SIM.

A SIM card is the actual place where the GSM network finds the telephone number of the user. The user can use the new terminal to receive calls, make calls, and use other subscriber services by the same telephone number by inserting the SIM into another GSM terminal.

The International Mobile Telephone Equipment Identity (IMEI) is used to uniquely identify the GSM terminal. The structure of IMEI is about 15 digits and is shown below in Fig. (**2**).

TAC (3 digits)	FAC (1 or 2 digits)	Serial No. (up to 11 digits)	1 Spare digit

Fig. (2). IMEI Structure (15 digits).

Type Approved Code (TAC): This is given to the terminal once it passes information tests.

Final Assembly Code (FAC): This identifies the final manufacture or assembly of MS units.

MS unit Serial number (11 digits) and 1 spare digit will be used for future agreements.

The SIM card contains the IMSI (International Mobile Subscriber Identity). The structure of IMSI is also up to 15 digits and is shown below in Fig. (3), which is used to identify the subscriber to the system and other information.

MCC (3 digits)	MNC (2 digits)	MSIC (up to 10 digits)

Fig. (3). IMSI Structure (15 digits).

Mobile Country Code (MCC): Used to identify the country where the GSM system operates.

Mobile Network Code (MNC): This uniquely identifies each cellular provider.

Mobile Subscriber Identification Code (MSIC): This uniquely identifies each customer of the provider.

Base Station Subsystem (BSS)

BSS comprises two parts: Base Transceiver Station (BTS) and Base Station Controller (BSC). BTS facilitates wireless communication between the user terminal and the network. Every tower will have a BTS. In large urban areas, there will potentially be many BSs deployed; thus, BSC manages the radio receivers for one or more cells.

Network Subsystem

The heart of mobile communication is the MSC. The MSC is associated with communication switching functions such as setting up user calls, call releasing, call recording, and call routing. The functionality of MSC includes support for registration, authentication, location updating, and handoff.

MSC has further components: Home Location Register (HLR) and Visitor Location Register (VLR), Equipment Identity Center (EIR), and Authentication Center (AuC). HLR is the Home Location Register. HLR is a database containing pertinent data regarding subscribers authorized to use a GSM network. If you are going to purchase a SIM in a specific area, then the entry is recorded in the database of HLR. HLR is like your home, which contains all the information, like your ID proofs and which plan you have opted for. There exists one HLR per GSM network; it is implemented as a distributed database. VLR is a Visitor Location Register. VLR is a database that contains the exact location of all mobile subscribers currently present in the service area of the MSC.

AuC authenticates mobile subscribers who want to connect to the network. EIR is a database that contains all subscribers who are allowed or banned on the network.

Equipment Identity Register (EIR)

It is a database that contains a list of all valid MSs on the network, each uniquely identified by its IMEI. Invalid MSs are those that have either been stolen or their operation is prohibited by masking their IMEI as invalid.

Public Switched Telephone Networks (PSTN)

PSTN is originally a network of fixed-line analog telephone systems, now entirely digital in its core networks and includes mobile and other networks as well as fixed telephones.

GSM Authentication and Security

Authentication involves two entities: SIM card in the MS and Authentication Centre (AUC). Each subscriber is given a secret key. Copies of this key are stored on the SIM card of the subscriber and in the AUC.

During authentication, the AUC generates a random number and sends it to the MS. Based on this number sent by the AUC and subscriber key, both MS and AUC use a ciphering algorithm called A3 to generate a signal response (SRES).

MS then sends the calculated SRES to AUC. If the number sent by mobile is calculated the same as the one by AUC, the subscriber is authenticated.

Both subscriber key and random number are used to perform encryption of traffic. The cipher key is produced by the A8 algorithm.

GSM FRAMES AND MULTI-FRAMES

As with other wireless networks, GSM encodes data into waves to send data over the wireless medium. The actual modulation scheme used is the Gaussian Minimum Shift Keying (GMSK). The available bandwidth of GSM (25MHz) is split into 124 carriers, each 200KHz wide. GSM uses a combination of TDMA and FDMA. One or more carrier frequencies are assigned to BS of GSM and each of these carriers is divided in the time domain.

Each period is called a slot and lasts 0.577 microseconds. A slot comprises the following parts, as shown in Fig. (**4**):

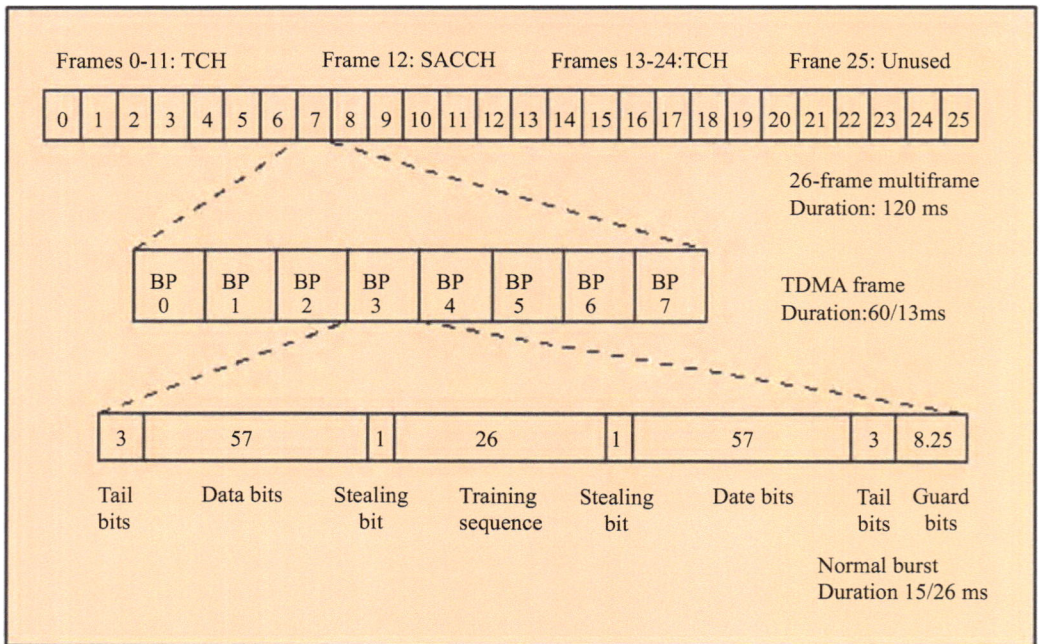

Fig. (4). GSM Frame format.

A GSM time slot comprises the following parts:

a. Head and Tail parts: These parts are 3 bits each used to ramp up and down the signal during signal transmission.
b. Training sequence: This part consists of 26 bits. This is used to enable MS and BS to learn the channel. The 26 bits training sequence constitutes a signal known to both BS and MS. The receiver will compare the incoming signal corresponding to the 26 bits training sequence and will use it to equalize the channel.
c. Stealing bit: These bits are used to identify whether the lot carries data or control information.
d. Traffic part: 57 bits long and carries either voice or data.
e. Guard band: 8 bits long and is essentially an empty space whose purpose is to provide guard intervals in the time domain to separate a slot from the previous slot to the next slot.

The normal burst is used to transmit information on traffic and control channels. The bursts are separated through guard bands. At the start and end of each burst are three tail bits, which are always set to logical "0". These bits fill a short period during which transmitter power is ramped up or down and during which no data transmission is possible. GSM burst is the transmission made in the time slot. The burst in GSM lasts 0.577 microseconds [2].

Normal Burst is as shown below:

2*(3 head bit + 57 data bits + 1 signalling bit) + 26 training sequence bit + 8.25 guard bit

GSM APPLICATIONS

GSM has plenty of applications due to its convenience and flexibility in usage. Some of the important applications are Telemetry Systems, Fleet management, Automatic meter reading, Mobile telephony, GSM-R, Remote control and fault reporting of DG sets, Value Added Services, *etc.*

SOLARCOM is a special telemetry unit with solar charging designed for use in extreme conditions without power supply options. Measuring modules are integrated into the unit. Transmission of measured data is realized *via* the GSM network.

Short message services are one of the very attractive services provided by GSM. Using this service, a maximum of 160 alphanumeric characters are sent or received *via* voice mail or fax mail earlier, but later, due to the advancements in technology, more than 160 alphanumeric characters can be transmitted.

GSM value-added service (VAS) is a popular telecommunications industry term for non-core **services**, or, in short, all **services** beyond standard voice calls and fax transmissions. However, it can be used in any **service** industry for **services** available at little or no cost to promote their primary business.

GSM GPRS Remote Control and Monitoring enables the user to control and monitor electronic devices using cell phones.

MOBILITY MANAGEMENT IN GSM

This is required whenever a mobile user is moving from one place to another. The purpose of mobility management is to check whether our network service is efficient or not. So, whenever the user moves from one place to another place, it follows a particular network, which means the network service should not be interrupted. Mobility management in GSM follows roughly 7 steps. Suppose the mobile user is at Node N1 (assuming the user is at Bombay) and is moving to a new place, say Node N2, in that place (assume the user is at Bengaluru). At the initial place, node N1 is connected to a Base station BS and is further connected to the Base Station switching Centre BSC. BSC is further connected to HLR and VLR. HLR and VLR are connected to the target Mobile Switching Centre (MSC). MSC is connected to target BSC, which is connected to target BS or node N2. This process of moving from Bombay (N1) to Bengaluru (N2) follows 7 steps to properly deliver the service:

   i. The user is at Bombay, *i.e.*, node N1.
  ii. Node N1 is connected to the base station, which is a relay.
 iii. The base station is then connected to BSC. Several other base stations may also be connected to BSC.
  iv. BSC is connected to HLR and VLR, which store the data of the customers. They may store data of other customers also.
   v. BSC is connected to MSC, which switches the data packets from one network to another.
  vi. The target BSC is connected to the MSC. MSC will switch the data of Node N1 from HLR and VLR to target BSC, target BS, and Node N2.
 vii. Whatever happens between Node N1 and source BS will now happen at Node N2 and target BS. So with the help of MSC, the data about Node N1 stored at HLR and VLR will get shifted to target BSC and further shifted to target BS. So the same communication that was happening at node N1 and source BS now gets shifted to node N2 connected to target BS.

GSM HANDOFF

If the mobile user moves to the coverage area of another BS, the radio link to the old BS is eventually disconnected, and the link to the new BS should be established. This is called automatic link handover or handoff. Handoff may happen in four different ways, as shown in Fig. (5).

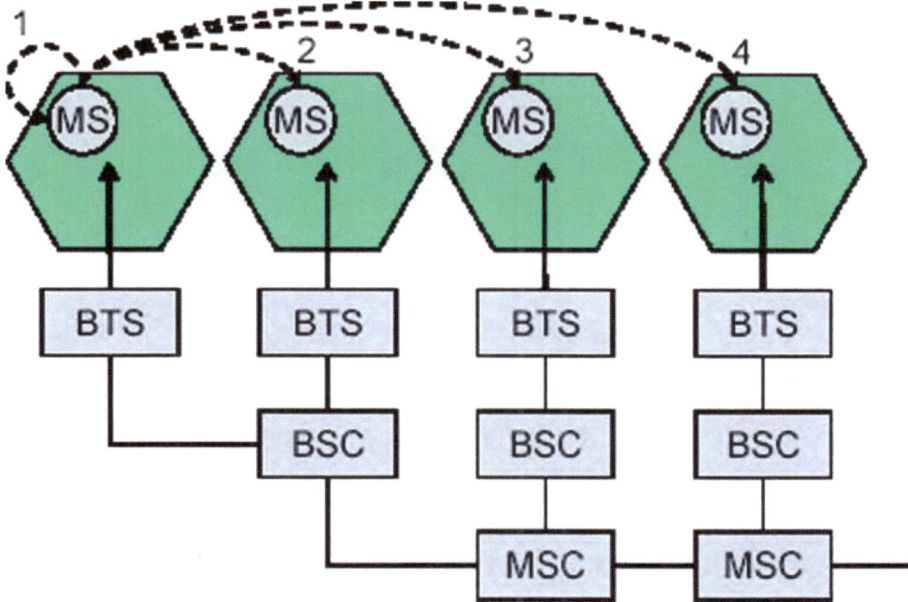

Fig. (5). Types of Handoffs in GSM. .

The first two types (1 and 2) are called internal handoffs, and the last 2 types (3 and 4) are called external handoffs. Handoff that happens within a cell due to narrowband interference is internal handoff. This involves only BSC. Here, BSC is responsible for finding the signal strength and allotting BS to the MS. The external handoff is initiated by MS or MSC.

3G CELLULAR NETWORKS

CDMA 2000

Evolution

GSM and CDMA network technologies are used all over the globe. GSM (Global System for Mobile Communications) was invented in 1990 in Europe by the GSM Association. CDMA (Code Division Multiple Access) is a proprietary standard that was launched by Qualcomm Inc. in the USA. It was 1995 when CDMA crossed the United States' boundaries and became an international standard. GSM is an international standard based on Time Division Multiple Access. It is used across the globe, especially in Europe, Asia, and the Middle East, while CDMA is restricted to a few Asian countries and the United States.

IS-95 was the first 'operating system' to use CDMA invented by Qualcomm. Its production began in 1995. At this point, this is still called 2G wireless known as a narrowband system. Later, the invention of CDMA2000 (WCDMA) and UMTS made it fully 3G systems. They both use CDMA known as wideband systems.

Working

CDMA is a fully digital wireless data transmission system. It is not designed for voice at all. CDMA uses special random numbers to encode bits of information. It allows multiple access by assigning different users different random numbers on the same channel. Users have control over a very wide channel bandwidth of 1.5 to 5 MHz. The only limit to the system is the computing power of the base station and its ability to separate noise from actual data.

With CDMA, every user is associated with a unique code for transmission. CDMA is a spread-spectrum multiple-access technique. Unlike FDMA, here, the user is not restricted to using a fixed frequency band; instead, the user can make use of any frequency band for transmission. Also, unlike TDMA, here, the user is not restricted from using the spectrum in a fixed time. So, with CDMA, simultaneous transmission from all the users is possible.

Suppose that there are two users at the transmission end, user A and user B. The messages generated by user A and user B are represented in terms of narrow-band signals in green and blue colors, respectively. Before transmitting these signals, they will be multiplied with a unique code. As shown in Fig. (6), after multiplying the narrow band signal with code A and code B, we can see the broadband signals for user A narrow band signal and user B narrow band signal, respectively. The same process continues if there exists an N number of users in the system. Note that code A is different from code B. After the conversion from narrowband signal to wideband signal, all these wideband signals will be transmitted over a radio spectrum. At the receiving end, if we want the original signal sent by user A, then the signal received can be decrypted using Code A (green color) used on the transmitter side. Doing so, a wide band signal gets converted to a narrow band signal again, which is the same as the transmitter signal. Similarly, the same procedure continues with other user's signals as well. The received narrowband signal gets further processed to do the data replication process.

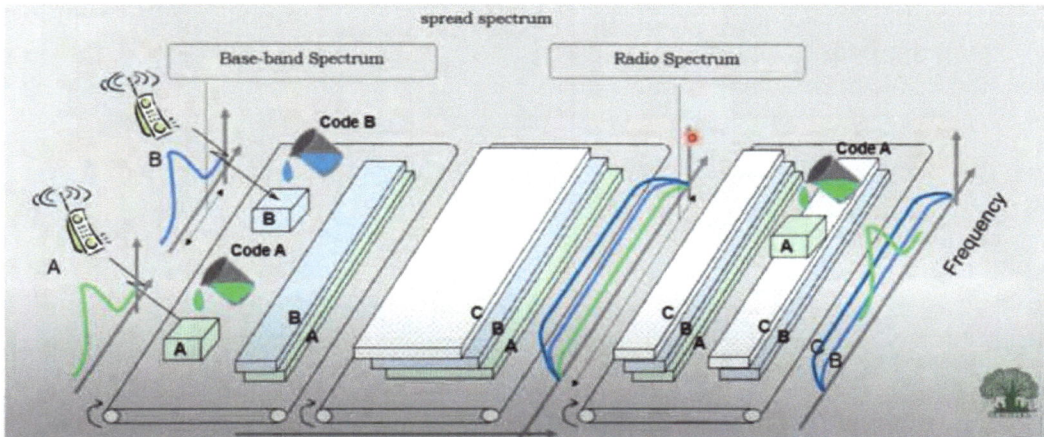

Fig. (6). CDMA working.

Fig. (7) shows an illustration of code division multiple access. The first row shows the data signal generated by a particular user, which is a narrow-band signal. After multiplying the narrow band signal with the pseudorandom code, the sample result is depicted in the second row. These are the wide-band signals or encoded signals that get transmitted over radio channels.

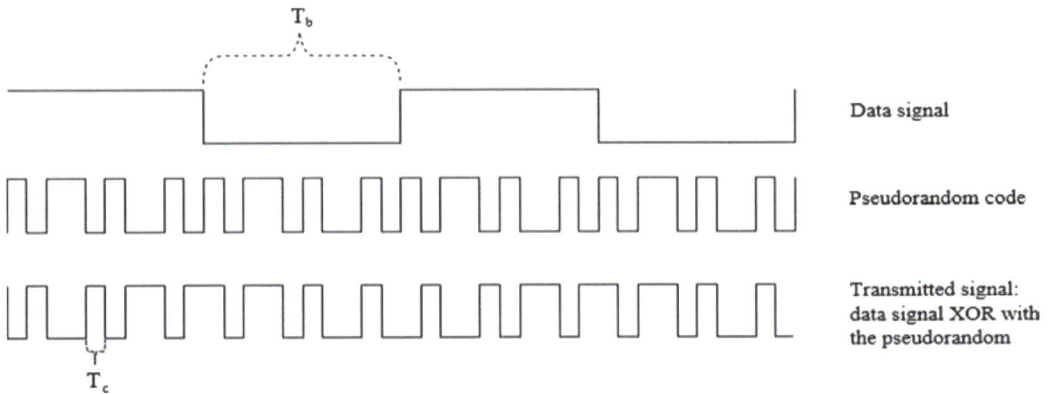

Fig. (7). Generation of a CDMA signal.

CDMA APPLICATIONS

CDMA has many advantages. Important ones are listed below:

  i. Can be used for short message transmission.
 ii. Used in the military for secret message transmission as the message generated is difficult to listen to, difficult to block, and even difficult to identify.

iii. Due to the broadband spectrum generation, CDMA can be used in wireless laptop modems.
iv. Used in radar and navigation.
v. Effectively works in personal communication.

WIDEBAND CODE DIVISION MULTIPLE ACCESS (WCDMA)

WCDMA, also known as W-CDMA, is a communications standard used in 3G mobile networks. Why do we call it WCDMA? The answer to this question is that the frequency channel that the mobile user can use in the uplink and the downlink would be 5 MHz each.

WCDMA is primarily designed for multimedia communication not only for voice communications. It supports higher bit rates, higher spectrum efficiency, and higher QoS compared to CDMA.

The processing procedure for WCDMA involves several steps, such as source coding, channel coding, spreading, modulation, and transmission at the transmitter end. Similarly, the reverse process at the receiver end involves reception, demodulation, dispreading, channel decoding, and source decoding. Finally, the signal is retrieved.

Source coding increases the transmission efficiency of the signal. Channel coding makes the transmission more reliable using error detection and error correction capabilities. Multi-level spreading techniques are introduced to overcome interference.

A sample spreading and de-spreading process is shown in Fig. (8).

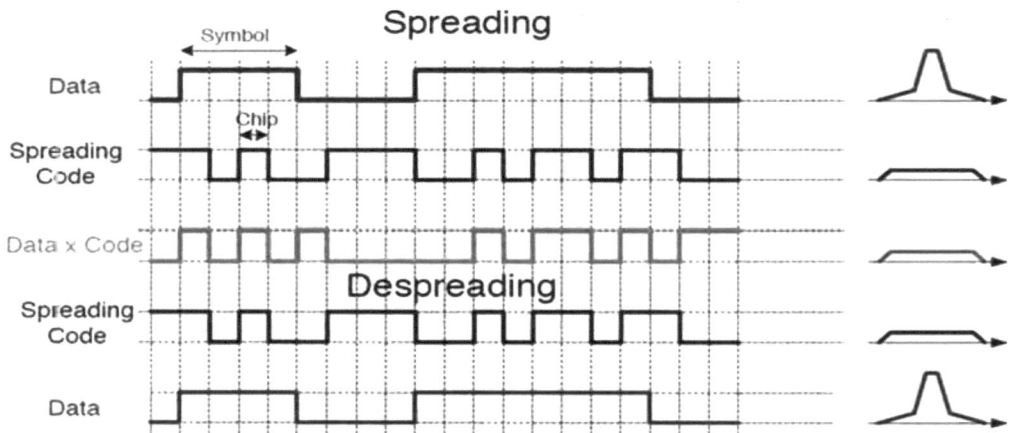

Fig. (8). Spreading and De-spreading of signal in WCDMA.

WCDMA supports both FDD and TDD modes of operation. In Frequency Division Duplex (FDD), separate 5 MHz carrier frequencies are used for uplink and downlink. In Time Division Duplex (TDD), only one 5 MHz is time-shared between uplink and downlink.

Table **1** explains the important differences between WCDMA and GSM technologies in terms of parameters such as bandwidth, frequency, power control, quality control, scheduling, *etc.*

Table 1. Comparison between WCDMA and GSM.

Parameters	WCDMA	GSM
Bandwidth	5 MHz	200 KHz
Power Control	1.5KHz for uplink and downlink	Lower
Frequency Diversity	Multipath diversity	Frequency Hopping
Quality Control	Dynamic Radio Resource Management	Network planning and dynamic channel allocation
Area of Coverage	Works throughout the world	Works only in European countries
Speed of communication	Works at high speed	Works at a slow speed

UMTS TRANSMISSION NETWORKS

UMTS (Universal Mobile Telecommunications Service) is a third-generation (3G) telecommunication system. UMTS, or 3G cellular system, is developed and maintained by the third group partnership project (3GPP), which is an organization that looks into the development of the global system. The basic aim of 3GPP is to provide higher data rates and good voice services. To achieve this, various new parameters have been inculcated into this 3G architecture. UMTS emerged out of the GSM standard and has a new air interface based on the WCDMA.

UMTS network architecture is shown in Fig. (**9**). It defines 3 main functional entities: User Equipment (UE), UMTS Radio Access Network (UTRAN), and the Core Network (CN). These 3 entities are connected with different interfaces.

Here, UE can be our mobile phone. The UE consists of a mobile phone and a SIM card. Mobile phones help us to receive and transmission of radio signals and the SIM card in the mobile phone helps us to connect to various networks. So, with the combination of mobile phones and SIM cards, users will be able to communicate with the various people in the system.

Fig. (9). UMTS network architecture [3].

The base station used in UMTS is called "Node B", which replaces BTS. It provides the radio link between the UE and the network. Since the access technology is different from GSM, Node B is capable of handling CDMA subscribers on the new frequency bands. Node B is the termination point between the air interface and the transmission network of the RAN. It is responsible for power control, reporting the measured values to RNC and converting the signals into a single data stream before it transmits to RNC.

The UTRAN part deals with radio-related issues while UMTS CN is responsible for managing session and mobility information at the same time as switching and routing data calls. The Radio Network Controller (RNC) is the main component in the Radio network system, and it controls the usage and reliability of radio resources. An RNC is like a BSC and is interfaced with data transport.

4G CELLULAR NETWORKS

4G is the fourth generation of the broadband cellular network, which is much faster than 3G. 4G supports interactive multimedia, voice, video, wireless

Internet, and other broadband services. Technologically, 4G is much different from 3G. It started around 2010. 4G is one of the most efficient and powerful wireless broadband systems compared to the other generations. The access technique that the 4G uses is OFDM (Orthogonal Frequency Division Multiflexing). Some of the important features of 4G cellular networks are listed below:

    i. Support interactive multimedia services such as teleconferencing.
    ii. Support high transfer rates.
    iii. Provide Internet access anywhere.
    iv. Provide sophisticated wireless services in terms of WLAN and Bluetooth technology.
    v. Deployment cost is less than previous cellular technology.
    vi. Enhanced scalability, low cost.
    vii. Scalability of mobile networks (>10 times the capacity of 3G).

4G Wireless Standards

There are two dominant 4G wireless standards, which are given below:

    i. LTE (Long Term Evolution): It has a data rate of 100-200 Mbps.
    ii. WiMAX (Worldwide Interoperability for Microwave Access): It also has a data rate of 100-200 Mbps.

3G *Versus* 4G

Table **2** shows the comparison of 3G and 4G networks in terms of important wireless network features such as speed, frequency band, bandwidth, switching design, access technology, roaming, *etc*.

Table 2. Comparing 3G with 4G.

Wireless Network Features	3G (including 5G)	4G
Technology used	IMT 2000, WCDMA	LTE, WiMAX
Speeds	3.1 Mbps	100 Mbps (or more)
Features	Multimedia, Video call	High-speed, Real-Time Streaming
Frequency Band	Dependent on country or continent (1800-2400 MHz)	Higher frequency bands (2-8 GHz)
Internet Service	Broadband	Ultra Broadband
Bandwidth	25 MHz	100 MHz (or more)
Core Network	Packet Network	IP-based
Carrier Frequency	5 MHz	15 MHz

(Table 2) cont.....

Wireless Network Features	3G (including 5G)	4G
Access Technologies	W-CDMA, Edge	OFDM
Applications	Video conferencing, Mobile TV, GPS	High-speed Applications, Mobile TV, Wearable devices
Roaming	Due to divergence in standards, suffers in roaming	Easy roaming

The following are some of the design challenges of 4G cellular networks:

- System Interoperability.
- Terminal bandwidth and battery life.
- Packet switched network.
- Varying quality of bandwidth for wireless access.
- Advanced base station: smart antenna and self-configuring.
- Higher data rates.

System Interoperability

- One of the most challenging problems facing the deployment of 4G technology is how to access different heterogeneous mobile and wireless networks.
- There are two possible architectures.
- Multimode Devices.
- Overlay Networks.

Multimode Devices Architecture

A single physical terminal has multiple interfaces to access the different wireless networks. The advantages of this architecture are improved call completion, expanded coverage area, and reliable coverage in case of network, link, or switch failure. One of the drawbacks of multimode devices is complexity in the hardware of the device. Fig. (**10**) depicts the sample multimode device architecture.

Overlay Network Architecture

In this architecture, the user accesses an overlay network consisting of several Access Points (AP). The functions of AP are to select a wireless network based on availability and user choices to store IPs of user, network, and devices. Some of the advantages of this architecture are that it simplifies the hardware of the device and supports single billing. However, this architecture has the disadvantage of having more network devices.

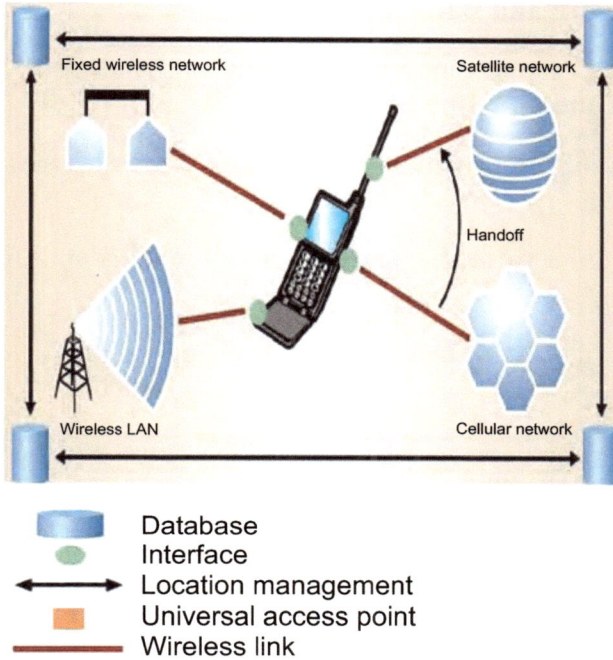

Fig. (10). Sample multimode devices architecture.

Fig. (**11**) shows sample overlay architecture.

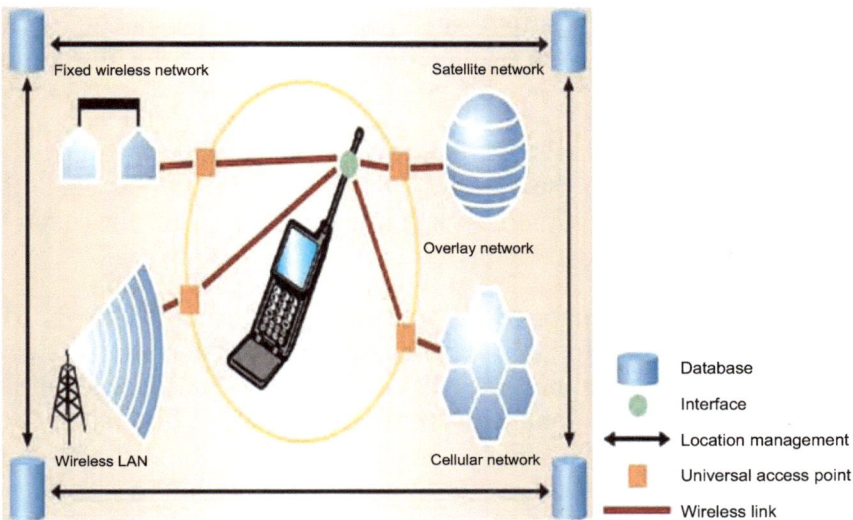

Fig. (11). Sample overlay architecture.

Terminal Bandwidth and Battery Life

4G cellular network should support a wide range of bandwidth ranging from kbps to 100mpbs, and battery life should be around 1 week.

Varying Quality of Bandwidth for Wireless Access Based on Geographic Location

The following are the various categories of bandwidths and the range in which they can be used:

Distribution layer: large cell size, rural, sparsely populated.

Cellular layer: small cell size.

Hot spot: short range within the building.

Personal network layer: very short range, Bluetooth Fixed layer.

OFDM

OFDM stands for Orthogonal Frequency Division Multiplexing. OFDM is a modulation scheme that is suitable for applications requiring high-data-rate transmission with reduced delays. Here, high-rate data streams are converted into several low-rate streams and are transmitted.

FDM and OFDM are the multiplexing techniques used mainly in the analog system. These techniques are distinguished depending on the spacing between the various subchannels (in the form of the composite signal) transmitted through a single channel.

So, in FDM, the message signals prevent noise by separating the signals with the help of the guard bands. On the contrary, the OFDM technique does not use a guard band; in fact, it allows the overlapping of the signals, thus enabling the better utilization of the provided bandwidth.

In the OFDM system, the data to be transmitted is assigned to the different individual carriers. The required phase and amplitude of the carrier are calculated based on the modulation scheme (like QPSK, 16 QAM, *etc.*); for example, if we are required to transmit 4-bit data, then we must choose 4 different carrier signals that are orthogonal to each other. Each carrier is assigned to a different bit, and its phase and amplitude are chosen according to the modulation scheme used in different cases. QPSK is one of the most popular linear modulation techniques. A

QPSK signal can be depicted using a two-dimensional constellation diagram with four points.

Fig. (**12a** and **b**) show the conventional and equivalent orthogonal multi-carrier techniques, respectively.

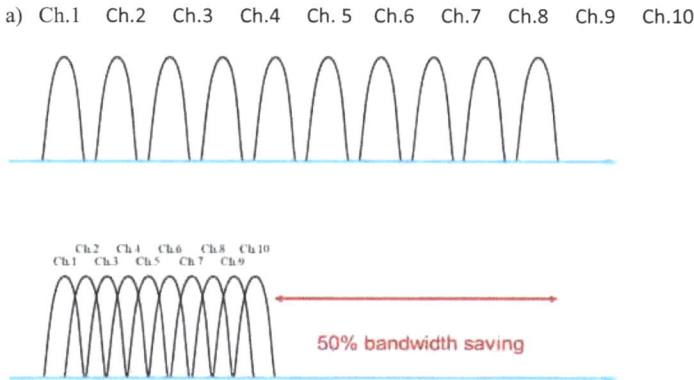

Fig. (12). (**a**) Conventional multicarrier technique (**b**) Orthogonal multicarrier techniques.

Fig. (**13**) shows the working of the OFDM Transmitter and OFDM Receiver.

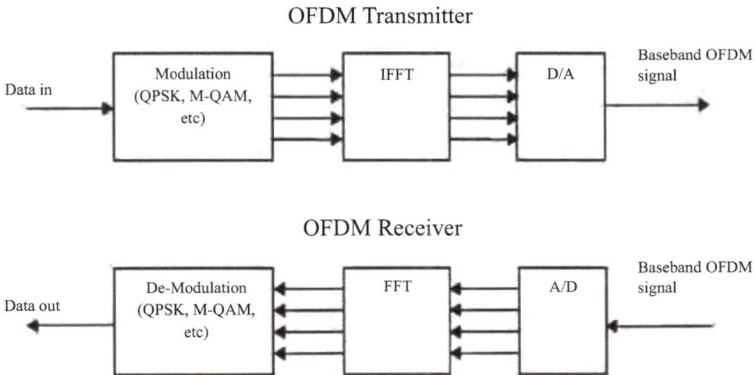

Fig. (13). OFDM Transmitter and OFDM Receiver.

Here, the Analog-to-Digital(A/D) converter converts the information signal to be transmitted to digital bits. The OFDM transmitter maps the digital bits into a sequence of PSK or QAM symbols, which are subsequently converted into parallel streams. At the transmitter, the IFFT (Inverse Fast Fourier Transform) algorithm is employed. Similarly, the FFT (Fast Fourier Transform) algorithm is employed at the receiver.

CONCLUDING REMARKS

This chapter describes the generations of cellular systems such as 1G, 2G, 3G, and 4G in terms of their architecture, working, access technologies, and characteristics. Also, each of these cellular systems is compared in terms of wireless network features.

EXERCISES

1. What types of access technologies are used for the following systems?
   a. AMPS (b) GSM (c) IMT 2000
2. Explain the following concerning GSM:
   i. Authentication and Security
   ii. Call set up to an MS
3. What is the need for OFDM? Explain the workings of the OFDM system with a neat block diagram.
4. Concerning cellular networks, explain Handoff strategy classification based on the nature of handoff.
5. Compare GSM and WCDMA in terms of 4 important parameters.
6. List the advantages and disadvantages of CDMA.
7. Compare 3G and 4G in terms of wireless network features.

REFERENCES

[1]   Wi. Stallings, "Wireless communications and networks", In: *Pearson Prentice Hall® is a trademark of Pearson Education* Inc, 2005.

[2]   P. Nicopolitidis, *Wireless Networks.,* John Wiley & sons, inc., publication, 2005.

[3]   Available from: https://www.rfwireless-world.com/Tutorials/UMTS-Network-Architecture.html

CHAPTER 3

Fixed Wireless Networks

Abstract: Fixed Wireless Networks are used to establish communication between two fixed locations *via* radio link or some other wireless means. Wireless Local Area Network (WLAN) is one of the popular Fixed Wireless Networks that can provide high-speed Internet access over wide area networks. WLAN can be configured into either infra-structured networks or an Ad hoc network. This chapter introduces WLAN technology based on the IEEE 802.11 standard. For wireless broadband services, IEEE 802.16 or WiMAX standards are introduced. Comparison of traditional wired networks with fixed wireless networks is also discussed based on important aspects such as speed, bandwidth, installation, cost, coverage, maintenance, *etc.* A sample use case that gives a basic idea about the creation of a Fixed Wireless Network is also illustrated.

Keywords: AD HOC, IEEE 802.11, IEEE 802.16, WLAN.

INTRODUCTION

Let us discuss the need for fixed wireless networks. Due to the advancement in VLSI (Very Large-Scale Integration) technology recently, the number of portable battery-operated equipment such as laptops, cellphones, PDA (Personal Digital Assistants), and palmtops has increased tremendously. These low-cost portable equipment are the driving force behind fixed wireless networks. Moreover, they have a lot of benefits; one of them is mobility. Due to this, people can communicate with each other while traveling and can attend conferences or meetings remotely from anywhere. Also, they have other benefits such as simple installation compared to their wired counterpart, minimal ownership cost, and easy scalability. One of the popular fixed wireless networks is WLAN.

WLAN offers several limitations as well as challenges. They are listed below:

i. Unreliable due to interference and noise: As communication happens through unguided media, unlike wired counterparts, there may be other devices communicating at the same frequency band that will interfere with the signal, which leads to low reliability due to the susceptibility of radio transmissions.
ii. Problem of fading: Signals can come through multiple paths that lead to fading due to fluctuations.

iii. Vulnerability to eavesdropping leads to security problems: Whenever someone is transmitting something through wireless media while broadcasting, unauthorized users can make improper use of it.

iv. Smaller data rate: The usage of spread spectrum in wireless networks leads to smaller data rates compared to wired LAN data rates.

The WLAN concept is simple. WLAN makes use of important standards, which are IEEE 802.11. Among various categories of protocols under IEEE 802.11, IEEE 802.11b is the most popular standard used nowadays. Like any other LAN technology, it consists of two layers: The physical layer and the data link layer. The Data Link Layer has two sub-layers: the Medium Access control layer and the Logical link control layer. IEEE 802.11b layered architecture is shown in Fig. (**1**).

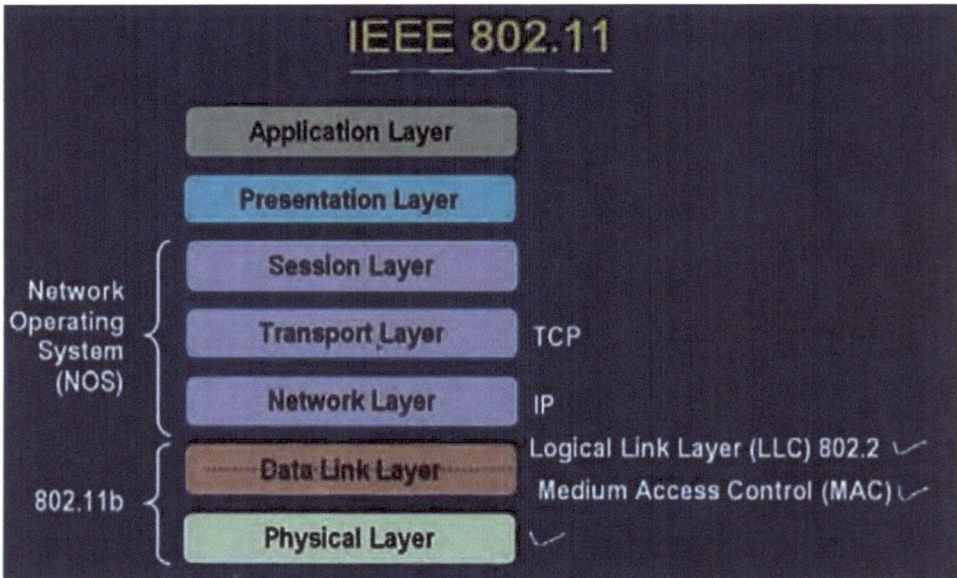

Fig. (1). IEEE 802.11 Layered architecture.

So essentially, the functionality of the bottom two layers, *i.e.*, the Physical layer and Medium Access layer, will be different in Wireless LAN, and the functionality of the upper layers, like TCP, IP, *etc.*, remains the same [1].

Important Parameters of WLAN

WLAN is characterized in terms of three important parameters: Topology, Transmission media, and Medium Access control techniques.

i. Transmission Media: Three different types of physical media are called Spread spectrum radio used in the 2.4GHz (2400 to 2483 MHz) ISM band, which is very popular and used by most household equipment. Spread Spectrum has 2 different approaches. They are FHSS (Frequency-hopping spread spectrum) and DSSS (Direct Sequence Spread Spectrum). The third approach is based on the infrared signal in the near visible range of 850 nanometers to 950 nanometers.

ii. Topology: IEEE 802.11 supports 2 types of BSS (Basic Service Sets). They are Ad hoc networks without access points and Infrastructure BSSs with access points.

iii. Medium Access Control: One of the challenges associated with Wireless LAN is that it is less reliable as it is more prone to interference.

WLAN Advantages

In the last two decades, the wired version of LAN has large-scale deployment and is widely used all over the globe. Until recently, wireless versions of LANs were not popular due to reasons such as low data rate, high cost, licensing requirements, and occupational safety concerns. This situation has changed significantly in the last couple of years.

WLAN has plenty of advantages. Important among them are listed below:

1. **Reduced Cost and Portable Equipment:** The equipment cost that is required for WLAN set-up has been reduced a lot due to the technological enhancements.
2. **Mobility:** With Wireless LAN, people can connect from any location without making use of cables and can attend meetings or conference calls even during traveling; the usage of WLAN has increased tremendously.
3. **Installation Speed and Simplicity:** Installation of Wireless LANs happens very easily and quickly compared to their wired counterpart. With wireless installation, there is no need for wiring for every workstation. This installation makes wireless LANs inherently flexible. Even the movement of the workstation can be done easily.
4. **Installation Flexibility:** Since wireless LAN can be installed anywhere, for example, in places where natural disasters have occurred, such as floods or earthquakes, there is a high level of flexibility and portability with this type of network.
5. **Reduced Cost of Ownership:** Even though the initial installation might require more expenditure on wireless connectivity for its hardware, it is surveyed that the overall installation expenses and life cycle costs can be significantly lower.

6. **Scalability:** As we can easily add any number of nodes to wireless LAN in a variety of topologies, Wireless LAN can be configured in the following two main topologies: Infrastructure and Ad hoc. It is represented in Fig. (2):

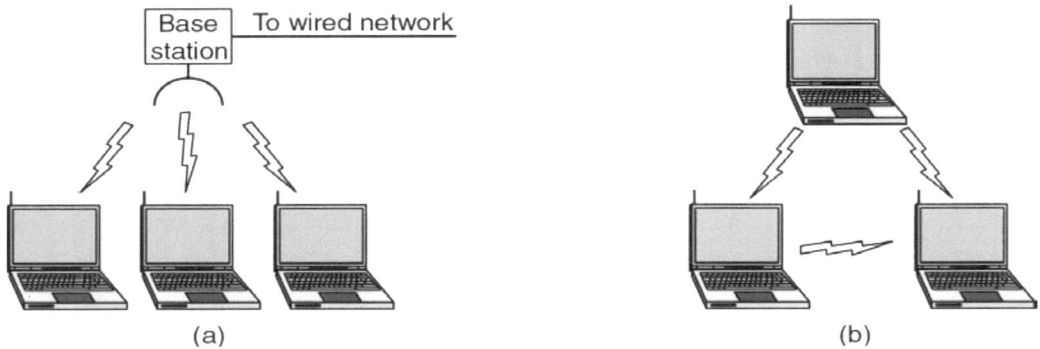

Fig. (2). (a) Wireless networking with a base station. (b) Ad hoc networking.

The first type, known as Infrastructure WLAN, makes use of a high-speed wired or wireless backbone. Here, the wireless channel is under the coordination of the base station. It makes use of a centralized MAC protocol. Access Point (AP) takes care of most functionality. If BS is used to interface the mobile nodes to a wired network, then it is called AP.

The second type of WLAN is called Ad hoc Network, which consists of a group of stations within the range of each other. It is referred to as Ad Hoc because these are created and maintained without any prior administrative arrangements.

IEEE 802.11a, b, and g

IEEE 802.11 protocol is extended in various directions. Initially, it was established in the year 1997, using a 2.4GHz frequency ISM band and data rates of 1 Mbps and 2 Mbps. It was extended to IEEE 802.11b during the year 1999. In this section, wireless LAN technology based on the IEEE 802.11 standard is introduced. The IEEE 802.3, commonly referred to as the Ethernet, is the most widely deployed member of the family, which is the predecessor of IEEE 802.11. IEEE 802.11 is commonly referred to as wireless Ethernet because of its close similarity with IEEE 802.3.

1. **IEEE 802.11a:** This is a successor of IEEE 802.11b. IEEE 802.11a uses an unlicensed 5GHz frequency band. It uses a special type of coding known as Orthogonal Frequency Division Multi-carrier (OFDM), which is very similar to FDMA with a little difference. IEEE 802.11a supports a wide variety of data

rates as high as 54 Mbps and also supports 6Mbps, 12Mbps, 24Mbps, and 34 Mbps. For 54 Mbps, the range is very small, typically 20-30 meters. For lower data rates, the range is 100 meters or more.

2. **IEEE 802.11b:** IEEE 802.11b is backward compatible with IEEE 802.11. and uses the same 2.4 GHz ISM frequency band as IEEE 802.11. It supports data rates of 5.5Mbps and 11Mbps using new coding techniques.

Two important coding techniques used with IEEE 802.11b are (i) Complementary coding Keying (CCK) modulation and (ii) Packet Binary Convolution Coding (PBCC). With these coding techniques, higher data rates, *i.e.*, 5.5Mbps and 11Mbps using the same ISM band, are possible.

IEEE 802.11b is very popular due to its backward compatibility with IEEE 802.11 standard. IEEE 802.11b uses Direct Frequency Spread Spectrum (DSSS).

3. IEEE 802.11g: It is a successor of 802.11b, and it is also backward compatible with IEEE 802.11b, whereas IEEE 802.11a is not compatible with IEEE 802.11b. The success of IEEE 802.11b led to another extension that supports higher data rates up to 22Mbps transmission. It retains backward compatibility with the popular 802.11b standard. IEEE 802.11g uses OFDM techniques.

802.11 Medium Access Control (MAC) sublayer of Wireless LAN

As in the case of wireless LAN, all stations that are not in the range of each other have to face two popular problems: Hidden Terminal Problem and Exposed Terminal Problem. These two problems are discussed in most of the literature [2] [3].

Hidden Terminal Problem

Two sender nodes out of range of each other transmit packets at the same time to the same receiver, resulting in collisions at the receiver. For example, as shown in Fig. (**3a**) node A wants to send to node B, but it cannot hear that node B is busy. Also, node C is not in the range of node A. So, in the case of the hidden station problem, wireless nodes have transmission ranges, and not all stations are in the same range as each other, *i.e.*, B is in the range of C, but it is not in the range of A. Here, a simple CSMA protocol will not work. Suppose C transmits to B, and if A senses the channel, it will not hear C's transmission and falsely conclude that A can begin a transmission to B.

Fig. (**3**) demonstrates the hidden and exposed terminal problem. Here, Terminal A sends a message to Terminal B. Terminal C cannot receive a message from A. C wants to send a message to B. C senses a "free" medium (Carrier Sense fails).

Collision occurs at B. A cannot detect this collision (Collision Detection fails) and continues with its transmission to B. A is "hidden" for C.

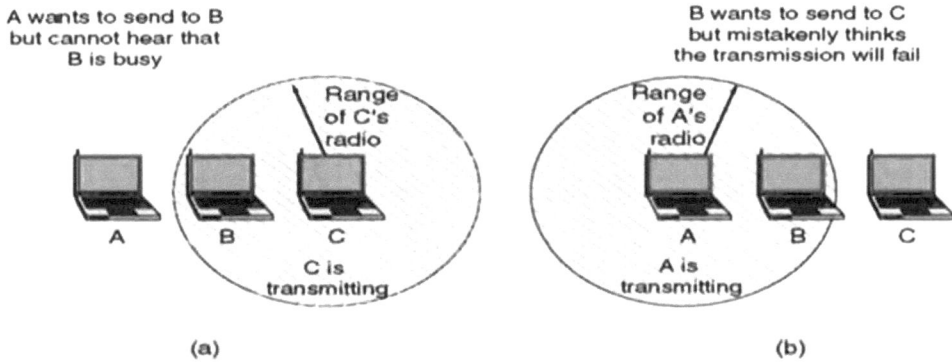

Fig. (3). (**a & b**) Hidden and Exposed Terminal Problem.

Exposed Terminal Problem

It is the inverse of the hidden station problem. Here, node B wants to transmit to node C and listens to the channel. When node B hears node as transmission, B falsely assumes that it cannot transmit to node C. This is depicted in Fig. (**3b**).

The primary operations of the IEEE 802.11 MAC sublayer are accessing the wireless medium, joining the network, and providing authentication and privacy, which is shown in Fig. (**4**):

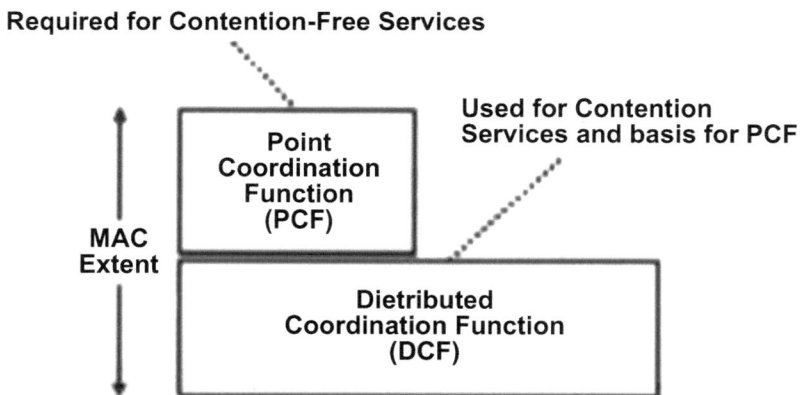

Fig. (4). WLAN IEEE 802.11 MAC sublayer.

MAC extent supports two different modes: Distributed Coordination Function (DCF) and Point Coordination Function (PCF). PCF sits on top of DCF. The purpose of PCF is to provide contention-free services. DCF is mainly based on the protocol Carrier Sense Multiple Access Collision Avoidance (CSMA/CA).

How does DCF work? It does not use any kind of central control, unlike Ethernet. Whereas, the ethernet uses a central control system that controls all devices. When DCF is used at IEEE 802.11 at the MAC layer, it makes use of CSMA/CA. The advantage here is that it avoids collision before it occurs. Both DCF and PCF make use of two modes of sensing: physical sensing and virtual sensing.

How does physical channel sensing work? Here, before the data needs to be transmitted, the channel gets sensed. Once it identifies that the channel is idle, it transmits the data to the channel. If the sender identifies that the channel is not idle, it waits until the channel becomes idle and then transmits the data through the channel. During the transmission of the data, the stations never sense the channel. Due to this, at any point in time, a collision may occur. Once the collision occurs, the collided stations will wait for a random amount of time until the ethernet binary exponent backoff algorithm gets executed. Once the channel is again idle, then only stations start transmitting the data. If the channel is idle, then the sender sends Ready to Send (RTS), informing them that the station is ready to send. When the receiver is ready to receive the data, it sends Clear to Send (CTS). If the receiver is not ready to receive the data, it runs a binary exponent backoff algorithm similar to the sender. This process keeps repeating.

WLAN Applications

  i. *Low Installation Cost:* Since WLAN does not require a cable connection, the cost of installation can be reduced.
 ii. *To extend the existing LAN:* WLANs are needed in a situation where flexible extension of existing infrastructure is needed; for example, in manufacturing plants and warehouses where extension of existing LAN is required. Suppose that there exist 2 wireless LANs located in 2 different nearby buildings separated by a road in between, they can be easily extended, as shown in Fig. (**5**). Whereas with wired LAN, it is very difficult or impossible to connect these two.
iii. *Ad hoc networking:* In certain applications, there is a sudden need for the deployment of network connections with limited or no infrastructure. For example, in a disaster situation, maintaining a network to communicate between people, an Ad hoc network can be immediately built.
 iv. *Nomadic Access*: It is an established connection between the portable terminal and LAN hub; for example, an employee wants to transfer data from his portable PC to the server in his office upon returning from a trip or meeting.

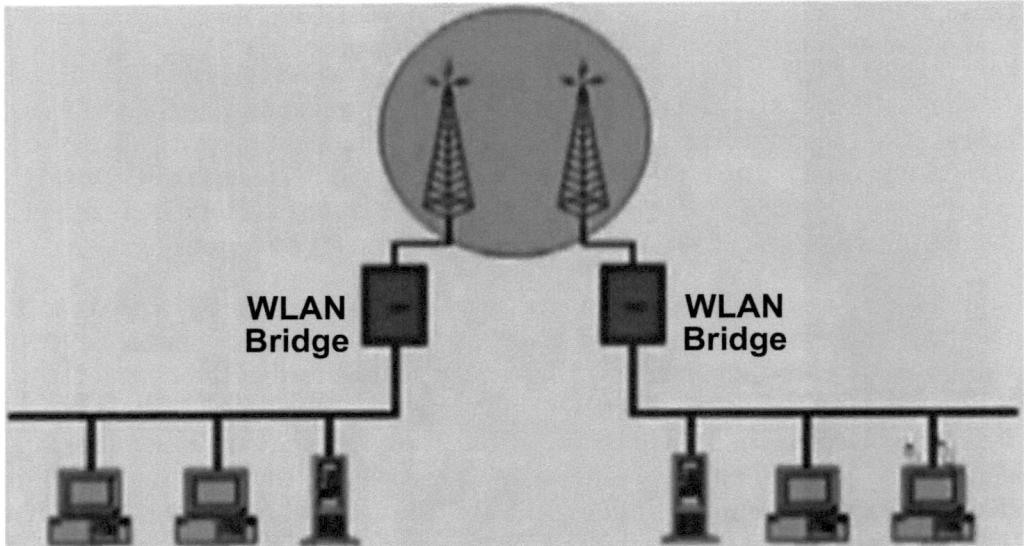

Fig. (5). Connecting Two WLANs.

WiMAX

WiMAX stands for Worldwide Interoperability for Microwave Access, and it comes under 4G wireless communication. The technical name for this group is IEEE 802.16. This group was formed in the year 1998 to form an air interface standard for broadband wireless applications that increase the wireless data rates that we have on Ethernet kind of broadband networks. It was initially focused on the development of Line-of-Sight (LOS) based point to multipoint wireless wideband networks. This original standardization was completed in the year 2001.

IEEE 802.16 standard subsequently produced IEEE 802.16a, which employed an OFDM-based physical layer that was used to support very high data rates. Early solutions based on IEEE 802.16 during 2004 were targeted for fixed wireless networks known as fixed WiMAX. In 2005, the IEEE 802.16 group approved an extended version of IEEE 802.16e, which was often referred to as mobile WiMAX.

WiMAX's physical layer is based on OFDM, which significantly enhances the signal strength and the data rates for broadband wireless access (BWA) such as Wireless LAN, Bluetooth, LTE, and so on, which are the 4G wireless networks.

Comparison of Traditional Wired Networks with Fixed Wireless Networks

Traditional wired networks with fixed wireless networks can be compared in terms of various aspects such as speed, cost, maintenance, *etc.*, which is shown in Table **1** below:

Table 1. Comparison between wired networks and wireless LAN.

-	Category of Networks	
Aspects	**Wired Networks**	**Wireless Networks**
1. Operating Speed	more	less
2. Bandwidth availability	more	limited
3. Installation	complex	easy
4. Cost	expensive	cheaper
5. Coverage range	limited	flexible
6. Interference	less	more
7. Reliability	better	limited
8. Mobility	difficult	easy

One of the benefits of a wireless network compared to a wired network is that it is easy to set up as there is no cable required. So, either a single person or a minimum number of people can deploy wireless networks. Another benefit is the mobility aspect of wireless networks. In a wired scenario, if we need to move a device, either a system or router, we need to unplug the cable from the location and plug it into the required location. This is not required in a wireless network, as it connects using radio frequency within the coverage area.

One of the limitations of wireless networks is that compared to wired networks, the speed is a bit less. With the wired network, we will get better throughput and high-speed data transfer rate. The speed of wireless networks also depends on what type of standard we use, such as either IEEE 802.11, IEEE 802.11 b, IEEE 802.11 g, or IEEE 802.11ac. Another limitation of wireless networks is that it is prone to some security issues.

Sample use Case Explaining the Deployment of Fixed Wireless Networks

Let us understand the basic idea of creating a Wi-Fi hotspot. Almost all the modern smartphones (Android or iPhones) that are available nowadays can be turned into Wi-Fi hotspots. We can switch on the hotspot in the mobile phone to turn on the Wi-Fi hotspot. This is called Wi-Fi tethering. Through this, we can wirelessly connect to any of our devices very quickly. However, there are some limitations to this approach, such as the battery of the smartphone drains quickly and the hotspot coverage area is limited. So, to cover large areas, proper Wi-Fi routers are required.

Sample FWA (Fixed Wireless Networks) use case is shown in Fig. (**6**):

Fixed Wireless Access (FWA): Indoor

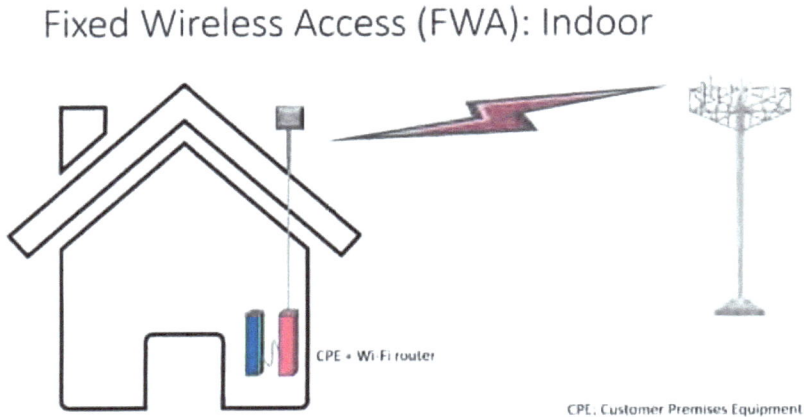

CPE • Wi-Fi router

CPE. Customer Premises Equipment

Fig. (6). Fixed Wireless Networks Use Case [4].

To have FWA indoors, first, we need an external high-gain antenna to get a reliable signal. This external antenna should be connected to the CPE (customer premises equipment). Different operators may adopt different methods for getting this connection. Once the signal is received by the external antenna, the Wi-Fi signal is switched off. This can even cover larger areas more than 100 meters. With one CPE, we can have Wi-Fi even for the entire building.

CONCLUDING REMARKS

In this chapter, an overview of WLAN in terms of infrastructure and ad hoc categories is discussed. Wireless LAN technology based on the IEEE 802.11 standard is introduced. A sample use case for Fixed Wireless Access is also illustrated.

EXERCISES

1. List and explain the two main categories of WLAN.
2. What do you mean by Ad hoc Network? How is it different from the infrastructure network? Why do we need an ad hoc network?
3. Distinguish between the Hidden Terminal Problem and the Exposed Terminal Problem.

4. How is the Hidden Terminal Problem overcome?

5. Distinguish between wireless networks and wired networks.

6. What are the benefits of wireless networks over wired networks?

7. What are the limitations of wireless networks over wired networks?

REFERENCES

[1]   Wi. Stallings "Wireless communications and networks", Pearson Prentice Hall® is a trademark of Pearson Education, Inc, 2005.

[2]   P. Nicopolitidis, "Wireless Networks", John Wiley & Sons, Inc., publication, 2005.

[3]   C. Siva Ram Murthy, "Ad hoc wireless networks: Architectures and protocols", In: . PHI, 2011.

[4]   Available from: Beginners: Fixed Wireless Access (FWA)

CHAPTER 4

Mobile Ad hoc Networks

Abstract: Mobile Ad hoc Network (MANET) is a category of Wireless Ad hoc Network. In MANET, topology keeps changing very frequently due to the mobility of nodes in the network. MANET faces a lot of challenges, such as the environment itself being decentralized, the medium being more error-prone, routing overhead, nodes operating with limited energy, and so on. There exist separate routing algorithms for Ad hoc networks, such as DSDV, DSR, AODV, CGSR, and WRP. VANET (Vehicular Ad hoc Network) is a special type of Intelligent Transport System (ITS), where the mobile nodes are cars, two-wheelers, trucks, buses, *etc.*

Keywords: AODV, CGSR, Challenges, DSDV, DSR, IEEE 802.11p, MANET, Mobility, VANET, WRP.

INTRODUCTION

Wireless Ad hoc networks are a broad class of networks. It is classified into pure wireless ad hoc networks, Mobile Ad hoc Networks (MANETs), Vehicular Ad hoc Networks(VANETs), and Wireless Sensor Networks (WSNs). In MANETs, some or all the nodes of the network are mobile or movable. Some of the important properties of MANETs are self-configure, self-heal, self-optimize, and self-protect. In MANETs, there are frequent link changes, which consequently lead to dynamic topological changes. Each node in MANETs acts as a router to forward the packets to other nodes in the network. Traditional routing protocols, which are used in wired networks, cannot be used with MANETs. IEEE 802.11p is an approved amendment to the IEEE 802.11 standard to add wireless access in vehicular environments (WAVE), a vehicular communication system. To work with VANETs, an enhanced version of IEEE 802.11p is developed.

MANET Characteristics

a. **Wireless:** Nodes in MANET operate in wireless media or wireless environment.
b. **Mobile:** Nodes are mobile in nature.
c. **No Structure:** There is no fixed structure for MANET. Topology keeps changing due to node mobility.

d. **Heterogeneous:** Nodes may be of different specifications.

e. **Autonomous Behavior:** MANETs can operate on their own, or they survive on their own whenever there is some kind of abnormality in the network.

f. **Dynamic Network Topology:** This means each node in the network can be joined or separated from the **network** anytime and anywhere.

g. **Energy-constrained:** Each node in MANET operates with a battery, so nodes have limited energy.

MANET Challenges

There exist some challenges in enabling the MANETs:

a. **Limited Bandwidth:** MANETs operate in the wireless medium. The availability of radio frequency bands is limited in the wireless medium.

b. **Dynamic Topology:** Due to the mobility of the nodes, topology keeps changing very frequently.

c. **Routing Overhead:** This is due to the periodic movement of nodes in the network. As and when nodes move, there is a routing overhead while discovering the new path to reach the destination and also maintaining the new routing information at every node.

d. **Hidden Terminal Problem:** In the case of MANETs, wireless nodes have transmission ranges, and not all stations are in the same range as each other, causing hidden station problems.

e. **Security Threats:** Due to the presence of features like open wireless medium, dynamic topology MANET is prone to security threats.

f. **Packet Losses Due to Transmission:** This is one of the significant problems that happen in the MANET while routing. This link breakage causes **packet loss** and **latency** problems in the network, and it degrades the performance. Each node in **MANET** acts both as a host and as a router.

MAC Protocols in MANETs

MAC protocol is essentially a set of rules or procedures that allow the efficient use of shared wireless medium by multiple users. In MANET, there may be a set of wireless nodes in the network that want to communicate with one another with multiple wireless paths. What is required here is to provide a mechanism in which these nodes will communicate with each other through a shared medium. So, MAC protocol in an Ad hoc network will help in doing so.

MAC protocol is concerned with per-link communication. This means that the nodes that are within the range of each other can communicate. MAC protocol needs some revision before using MANETs due to the following issues:

a. **Lack of Centralized Control:** Here the nodes do not have a complete view of the network, and there is a requirement for complete coordination to avoid collision between the packets sent by nodes.

b. **Nodes are Mobile:** Due to the movement of nodes in MANET, topology keeps changing.

c. **Nodes are Resource Constraints:** Due to limited energy available at the nodes in MANETs, we cannot run complicated algorithms.

d. **Wireless Channels are not Reliable:** Wireless channels are more prone to errors compared to their wired counterparts. These channels suffer from path loss, fading, and interference.

e. **Have Limited Channel Bandwidth:** MANETs have limited channel bandwidth. So, different nodes should share the bandwidth among them for communication.

MAC protocols are broadly classified under two headings:

Contention-based MAC Protocols

Here, the nodes are about to contend or compete to transmit the data to one or other nodes in the network, and there are no QoS guarantees. This means there is no guaranteed access to the channel. These protocols are further classified into sender-initiated protocols and receiver-initiated protocols.

i. Sender-initiated protocols: In sender-initiated protocols, more than one control packet is needed. So basically, the sender, instead of directly sending the data, sends the RTS/CTS(Request to send/Clear to send). Sender-initiated protocols are classified into Single-channel protocols and Multiple-channel protocols.

Examples of Single channel protocols: Multiple Access with Collision Avoidance (MACA) and Multiple Access with Collision Avoidance for Wireless (MACAW).

Examples of Multi-channel protocols: BTMA (Busy Tone Multiple Access) and DBTMA (Dual Busy Tone Multiple Access).

ii. Receiver-initiated protocols: In receiver-initiated protocols, the receiver initially does not know whether the sender has some data to send. The only way to know this is by periodically polling the sender. So here, only one control packet is used. The protocols under this category are Multiple Access Collision Avoidance By Invitation (MACA-BI) and Receiver-Initiated Busy-Tone Multiple Access (RI-BTMA).

Contention-based MAC Protocols with Reservation Mechanism

These protocols provide some bandwidth reservation priority. So they can provide QoS support. Contention-based MAC protocols with reservation mechanisms are further classified into Synchronous and Asynchronous protocols.

i. Synchronous protocols: Here, as the name suggests all the nodes are synchronous to the same channel. That means all the nodes follow the same timer or master timer. So, centralized coordination is needed.

Examples of Synchronous protocols: Hop Reservation Multiple Access (HRMA).

i. Asynchronous protocols: Unlike synchronous protocols, here, the nodes do not follow the same timer. This protocol follows a distributed mechanism to coordinate the channel access. The protocols under this category are MACA with piggy-backed reservation (MACA/PR) and reservation MAC (RTMAC).

Contention-based MAC Protocols with a Scheduling Mechanism

These protocols ensure some kind of fairness by enforcing priority among the flaws of packets between different nodes in the network. Contention-based protocol with scheduling needs packet scheduling at the nodes or scheduling of nodes for the channel access.

The protocols under this category are distributed priority scheduling

(DPS) and Distributed laxity-based priority scheduling (**DLPS**).

Problem of using CSMA in MANETs

CSMA is one of the well-known contention protocols used in MANETs. Some of the problems of using CSMA in MANETs are:

a. Hidden Terminal Problem: This means that if 2 nodes are hidden from each other, both want to send a packet to a common sender. Since both nodes are hidden from each other, they may send packets to the same receiver at the same time. This may cause a collision at the receiver's end, that is because both senders are unaware that they are sending packets to the same receiver at the same time. Consider Fig. (**1**), which shows the hidden terminal problem:

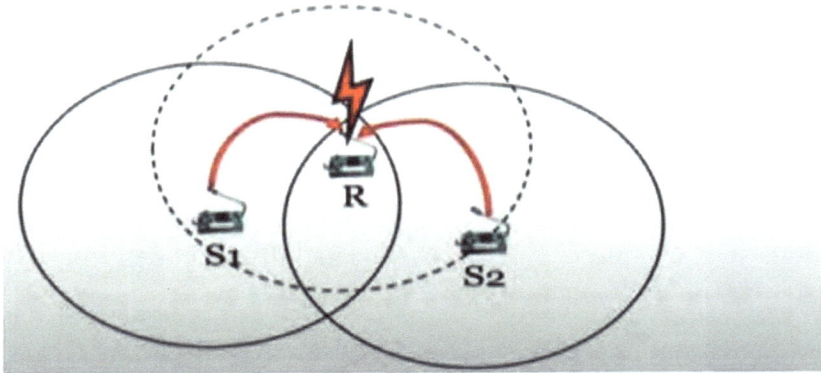

Fig. (1). Hidden Terminal Problem.

Here, nodes S1 and S2 are not within the range and are transmitting packets at the same time to node R. However, S1 and R are in the same transmission range; similarly, S2 and R are in the same transmission range of each other. There is a possibility that S1 and S2 may transmit packets to node R at the same time. This may cause collision problems in the network known as hidden terminal problems.

b. Exposed Terminal Problem: This is the inability of the node, which is blocked due to transmission by a nearby transmitting node, to transmit to another node. Fig. (2) shows the exposed terminal problem. Here, unlike the previous figure, there exist two receiver nodes, R1 and R2. As shown in the figure, Node S1 is within the transmission range of R1, Node S2 is within the transmission range of R2, and Node S1 is within the transmission range of S2. Node S1 sends a packet to node R1, and node S2 tries to send a packet to node R2. Since S1 and S2 are within the transmission range of each other, node S2 is exposed to transmit packets to R2. This is because S1 is within the transmission range of S2. S2 feels that there is another transmission happening and is going to differ in its transmission. This is known as the exposed terminal problem [1].

ROUTING IN AD HOC NETWORKS

Due to the unique features of Ad Hoc Networks, such as frequent topological changes, node mobility routing algorithms designed for wired networks might not work for these networks. Also, there are chances of variation in link capacity continuously due to noise, interference, and fading [2].

Traditional routing protocols may not work for routing in Ad Hoc networks due to the challenges that are posed by MANETs. One of the major challenges posed is the multi-hop nature of this network. Other challenges are the environment in which MANET operates, *i.e.*, they operate in a highly mobile as well as decentralized or distributed environment. There may be a lot of security-related concerns as the environment itself may be lossy compared to other wireless networks. So Ad Hoc network makes use of separate sets of routing protocols such as DSDV, DSR, WRP, AODV, *etc*. In MANET, each node has equal responsibility, *i.e.*, every node acts as a node as well as a router.

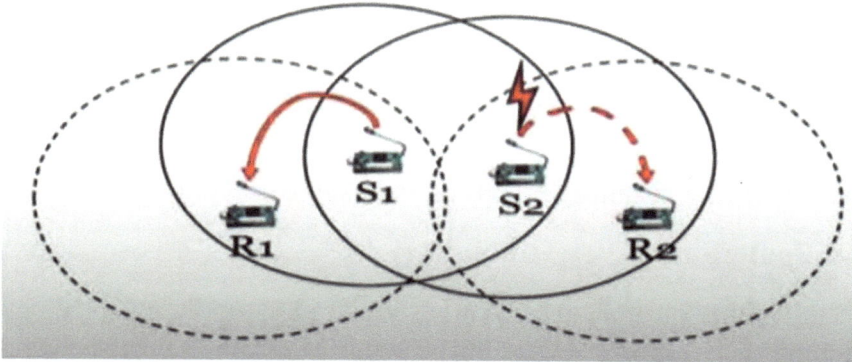

Fig. (2). Exposed Terminal Problem.

There are some challenges to be faced with respect to routing in mobile ad hoc networks. Firstly, one of the major challenges for routing in MANETs is that it is imposed by resource-constrained nodes and the mobility of the nodes participating in the network. As there is no fixed infrastructure in MANETs, each node is considered a host as well as a router.

Let us consider a scenario where there are 4 nodes in a MANET, as shown in Fig. (**3**):

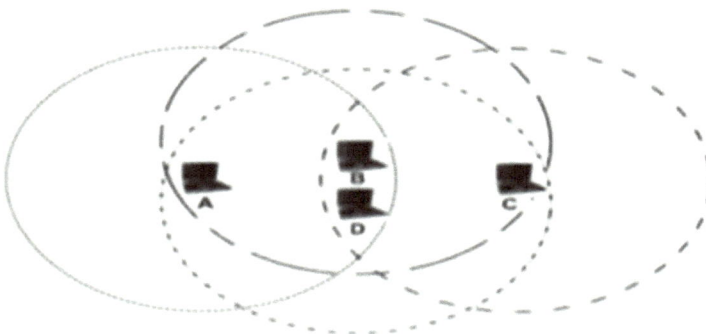

Fig. (3). Sample MANET with 4 nodes.

As per the above MANET, to send the packet from source Node A to destination node C, there are 4 different paths available: A-B-C, A-D-C, A-B-D-C, or A-D-B-C. Here, an efficient routing mechanism is needed to route a packet from node A to node C. The scenario worsens further if more nodes are added to this network because there may be a larger number of paths to send a packet from node A to node C. The routing process decides which path is to be used to transmit a packet from one node to another.

There have been various routing protocols proposed for Ad hoc networks, which are broadly classified under two headings: Proactive and Reactive. Another category is the Hybrid routing protocols, which is a combination of proactive and reactive routing protocols. Based on the delivery of packets, routing protocols are classified into Unicast Routing Protocols and Multicast Routing Protocols.

Proactive Routing

In proactive routing, protocols continuously learn the topology of the network by exchanging the topological information among the nodes in the network. Another name given to this protocol is the Table-Driven Routing protocol. Here, on receiving a request, there is no need to explore a path as the protocol proactively maintains topology information of all nodes in the network. In the routing table, information such as the next hop to that particular node in the network, sequence number, flag, *etc.*, gets stored. Proactive routing protocols are like the traditional Internet routing protocols. As the name suggests, in the routing table of every node, the information gets updated periodically. Examples of proactive routing algorithms are Wireless Routing Protocol (WRP), Destination Sequence Distance Vector (DSDV), and Cluster Head Gateway Switch Routing (CGSR).

Reactive Routing

In a reactive routing protocol, on receiving a request, it explores the possible routes to the destination node. Here, there is no periodic transmission of topological information of the network, unlike proactive routing protocols. Another name given to reactive routing protocol is on-demand routing protocol, which means whenever there is a need for the path, they are going to discover the path to the destination. This path is used to transmit the packet to the destination if the path is useful; otherwise, the protocol repeats the route discovery to find the suitable path to the destination. Dynamic Source Routing (DSR) and Ad hoc On-demand Distance Vector routing (AODV) are examples of reactive routing protocols for mobile ad hoc networks.

The Destination Sequence Distance Vector (DSDV) Routing Protocol

Destination Sequence Distance Vector (DSDV) is a proactive routing protocol and is based on the traditional Bellman-Ford algorithm with some modifications. Here, each mobile node maintains a routing table, and this routing table contains a list of all destinations and the total number of hops to reach this destination node. Each routing table is tagged with a sequence number that originates from the destination node. These sequence numbers ensure that the packets that arrive at a particular node are not stale and there is a time reference so that the latest version of the packet received is going to be taken. If there is any significant new change to the routing information, the updates are transmitted immediately. Here, the routes must be updated periodically by maintaining the topological information of the network. DSDV requires each mobile node in the network to advertise its routing table to its current neighbors. The advertisement is done either by broadcasting or by multicasting.

A sample table entry of the DSDV protocol is shown in Table **1**:

Table 1. Sample DSDV routing table.

Destination	Next	Metric	Seq. No.	Install Time	Stable Data
A	A	0	A-550	001000	Ptr_A
B	B	1	B-102	001200	Ptr_B
C	B	3	C-588	001200	Ptr_C

Fig. (**4**) shows how route advertisement is sent from node B to other nodes.

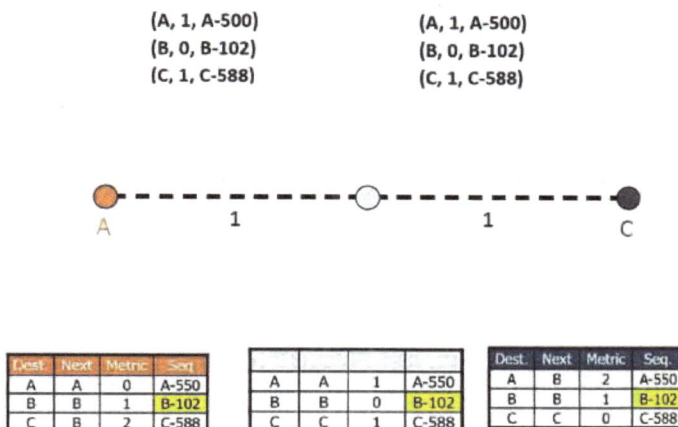

Fig. (4). Route advertisement is sent from node B.

Wireless Routing Protocol (WRP)

The Wireless Routing Protocol (WRP) belongs to the general class of path-finding algorithms. It uses the distributed shortest path algorithm that calculates the length and second to last hop of the shortest path to each destination. Each node maintains a distance table, routing table, link cost table, and message retransmission list.

A distance table of node X contains the distance of each destination node Y *via* each neighbor Z of node X and the predecessor node reported by Z. The routing table of node X is a vector with an entry for each known destination Y, which specifies the identifier of destination Y, distance to destination Y, predecessor of shortest path to Y, successor of chosen shortest path to Y, and a tag to identify whether a path is valid or not. Storing predecessors and successors in a routing table is beneficial to detect loops and avoid count-to-infinity problems.

The link cost table contains the cost of relaying information through each neighbor Z and the number of update periods that have elapsed. The message retransmission list contains information on the neighbors of a node from which an acknowledged update message is not received, hence retransmitting the update message to the neighbor [3].

Compared to DSDV, WRP incurs more overhead as it requires maintaining four tables and needs more energy.

The Dynamic Source Routing (DSR) Protocol

This routing protocol falls under the reactive routing protocol. As the name suggests, DSR is a source routing protocol. DSR allows nodes in a MANET to dynamically discover a source route across multiple network hops to any destination. Here, mobile nodes are required to maintain route caches of known routes. The route cache is updated when there is any new route known for a particular entry. Routing in DSR is achieved using two phases: Route Discovery and Route Maintenance.

When a mobile node has a packet to send to some destination, it first consults its route cache to check whether it has a route to that destination or not. If there is already an entry for that destination, it will use this route to send the packet. If the node does not have a route, it initiates route discovery by broadcasting a Route Request packet. This Route Request contains the destination address, source address, and unique identification number. The Route Reply is generated by the destination or an intermediate node when it knows how to reach the destination. Once the route is discovered, it is used, maintained, and used further for routing all different packets until the route cache is updated or until the routes that are identified seem to be invalid. This process is called the Route Discovery process [3]. The creation of the Route Record in DSR is shown in Fig. (**5**).

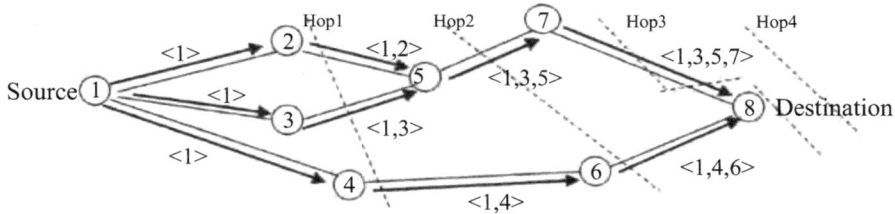

(a) Building Record Route During Route Discovery

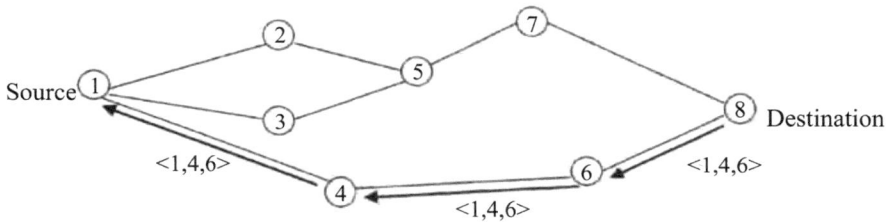

(b) Propagation of Route Reply with Route Record

Fig. (5). DSR Route Discovery and Maintenance.

In Fig. (**5a**), Route discovery to reach the packet from source node 1 to destination node 8 takes place. The route request RREQ packet gets broadcasted from the source node to the intermediate node, for example, nodes 2, 3, and 4 initially. If the destination is not reached again from the intermediate nodes, broadcast RREQ packets to other reachable nodes, for example, nodes 5 and 6, until the destination is reached. Here, at destination node 8, finally 2 paths <1,3,5,7,8> and <1,4,6,8> will be available. It stores these 2 routes in its route cache. In case any one of the paths gets damaged, then another path will be utilized for data transmission. DSR is powerful due to its cache. But its design is complex. Once all paths fail, a new route discovery process gets initiated. Once a route or path is discovered, the route reply packet will be unicasted from the destination node to the source node, having the path from the source node to the destination.

The Ad Hoc On-demand Distance Vector Routing (AODV) Protocol

AODV is an example of reactive routing protocol, which means whenever a node wants to transmit the packet to the destination, it starts searching for a route. Its work is similar to the working of the DSR routing protocol. This means that it operates in two phases: Route discovery and Route maintenance. Unlike DSR routing, the AODV source node will not carry a complete path. In AODV, each node only knows its previous and next hop information. Each node maintains its route cache.

To find the route, the route discovery process gets initiated by the node by broadcasting a Route Request (RREQ) packet to its immediate neighbors. This RREQ packet contains fields such as source address, destination address, recent sequence number, broadcast ID, hop count, *etc.* Once the neighboring node receives RREQ, it further broadcasts to its neighbor until it reaches the corresponding destination. Once a destination is reached, a path is obtained. There are chances of getting more than one path to the destination; in such cases, the path with minimum hops is selected to transmit the packet to the destination. The path that is identified as a path to reach to destination is then sent by using a Route Reply (RREP) message by unicast from the destination to the source node. Fig. (**6**) shows the working of the AODV protocol.

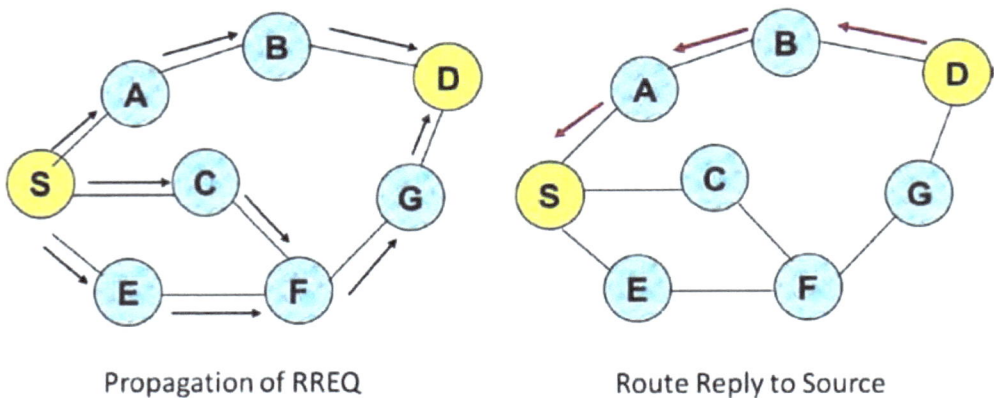

Propagation of RREQ   Route Reply to Source

Fig. (6). AODV Route Discovery.

A node is considered active if it participates in forwarding the packets. Link failures are known to all active nodes using Route Error (RERR) messages (destination sequence numbers are also updated). When a node cannot forward a packet toward a destination, it generates a RERR message, increases the sequence number for the destination, and includes this incremented destination sequence number in the RERR message. When a source receives the RERR, it initiates a new route discovery process for the destination using a sequence number equal to or greater than the destination sequence number in the RERR message [3].

VANETs (IEEE 802.11p)

A vehicular Ad hoc Network (VANET) is a kind of Ad hoc network where communication happens through the nodes within the vehicles during traveling. The primary purpose of VANETs is to provide road safety to drivers by providing dangerous alerts. Here, an Ad hoc network is formed by different vehicles that are moving on the road. In VANET, each vehicle wants to communicate with one another with the help of electronic equipment, which is known as an On-Board Unit (OBU), and these OBUs of these vehicles can talk to a device known as a Roadside Access Point (RSAP) or Roadside Access Unit (RSU). RSAPs are like access points but are installed on the roadside. With the help of this OBU, each of these vehicles can talk to each other. So, with this setup, we can have 2 possible communications: one between vehicles Vehicle to Vehicle (V2V) and another between vehicle and roadside unit *i.e.* Vehicle to Infrastructure (V2I).

VANETs are very useful because they perform spontaneous data exchange between vehicles. So, VANETs can be used in various applications as it is possible to track activities on the highway; sudden vehicle accidents have happened, which were known to nearby vehicles on the road from far. Another application may be to provide some services for the drivers so that they get more comfort while driving.

Even though VANETs look similar, MANETs are slightly different from MANETs in terms of traffic patterns. Unlike MANETs, the traffic pattern with VANETs is predictable, and nodes operate at very high mobility [3].

There are two important components in VANETs:

a. OBUs of the VANET help in collecting data from various sensors and can communicate with other OBUs.
b. RSUs help in enabling communication with outside networks.

Communication technology in VANETs, known as Wireless Access in Vehicular Environment (WAVE), supports multi-hop communication between vehicles. Different standards have been proposed for VANETs, such as IEEE 1609.2, commonly known as IEEE 802.11p, which is typically used for empowering VANETs. More recent work on IEEE 802.11 for Intelligent Transportation Systems and performance evaluation of enhancement of OFDM-based IEEE 802.11p is available in recent papers [4, 5].

CONCLUDING REMARKS

In this chapter, an overview of MANET in terms of infrastructure and ad hoc categories is discussed. Also, routing in an Ad hoc network is explained in terms of various algorithms by taking some sample networks. IEEE 802.11p, an approved amendment to the IEEE 802.11 standard, which is suitable for VANET, is also discussed.

EXERCISES

1. What do you mean by Ad hoc Network? How is it different from the infrastructure network? Why do we need an Ad hoc network?
2. Distinguish between proactive and reactive routing protocols.
3. What is the problem of traditional distance vector routing protocol? How does DSDV solve this problem?
4. Explain the working of the following routing protocols with neat diagrams:
      i. Dynamic Source Routing
     ii. Ad hoc On-demand Distance Vector Routing
5. Distinguish between MANET and VANET.
6. Describe the working of IEEE 802.11p for VANETs.

REFERENCES

[1]   P. Nicopolitidis, "Wireless networks", john wiley & sons, inc., publication, 2005.

[2]   C. Siva Ram Murthy, "Ad Hoc wireless networks: architectures and protocols", In: . PHI, 2011.

[3]   S. Misra, I. Woungang, and S.C. Misra, *Guide to Wireless Ad hoc Networks.* Springer: UK, 2008.

[4]   F. Arena, G. Pau, and A. Severino, "A review on IEEE 802.11p for intelligent transportation systems", *Journal of Sensor and Actuator Networks,* 2020.
   [http://dx.doi.org/10.3390/jsan9020022]

[5]   M. Abdelgadir and R.A. Saeed, "Evaluation of performance enhancement of OFDM based on cross layer design (CLD) IEEE 802.11p standard for vehicular ad-hoc networks (VANETs), city scenario", *International Journal of Signal Processing Systems,* 2020.

CHAPTER 5

Wireless Personal Area Network

Abstract: Wireless Personal Area Network (WPAN) or IEEE 802.15.4 standard defines the medium access control and physical layer specifications for low data rate wireless connectivity, interconnecting fixed or moving portable devices with low or no battery. A WPAN transmits data among devices such as laptops, smartphones, tablets, and personal digital assistants. IEEE 802.15.4 is a base on which several standards, such as ZigBee, Bluetooth, WSN, WISN, *etc.*, are built and can be used based on various applications.

Keywords: Bluetooth, WISN, WSN, WPAN, ZigBee.

INTRODUCTION

Wireless personal area networks (WPANs) are used by several technologies such as ZigBee, Bluetooth, 6LowPAN, Wireless HART, WSN, WISN, MiWi, ISA 100.11a *etc.*, as shown in Fig. (**1**). If we purchase any of the products of IEEE 802.15.4, then we will never hear about IEEE 802.15.4; instead, we can hear about the products ZigBee, 6LowPAN, *etc.* Among all these technologies, the most popular one is ZigBee. IEEE 802.15.4 is a low-rate wireless personal area network (LR-WPAN). As the name indicates, it cannot be used for high-speed data transmission. It can be used with IoT devices. It makes use of a 2.4GHz frequency band, which is the same band used by Bluetooth and Wi-Fi. In this band, there are 80MHz available, so we can use sixteen 5 MHz channels out of it. We can get 250kbps out of that but we get only 50kbps upon the application. This limited data rate is due to the overhead at the wireless channel.

IEEE 802.15.4 makes use of the direct frequency spread spectrum technique for spreading the narrow band signal to a broad range of frequencies, and Carrier sense multiple access/collision avoidance (CSMA/CA) is used to minimize the collision when two or more stations send their signals over a data link layer. IEEE 802.15.4 is used for lower data rates, short distances, and lower energy utilization.

Fig. (1). WPAN standards.

Bluetooth (IEEE 802.15.4)

There are multiple ways to transmit data from one person to another . For example, data can be transmitted from one person to another either by sending it through WhatsApp or by emailing the data using the Internet. Rather than making use of the Internet to transmit data between the nodes, if we want to transmit data from one node to another wirelessly without the Internet, then both nodes should have Bluetooth adapters.

Bluetooth is a wireless technology standard used for exchanging information between fixed and mobile devices over a short distance using short wavelength Ultra High Frequency (UHF) radio waves in the ISM radio bands from 2.4GHz to 2.485 GHz, thus building Personal Area Networks. An industry consortium specifies Bluetooth called the Bluetooth Special Interest Group (SIG). This SIG specifies an entire suite of protocols that go beyond the link layer to define application protocols, which are called profiles for a range of applications. There exists a separate profile for separate applications. For example, we need a profile to synchronize PDA with personal computers or we may need a profile to give mobile computer access to a Wired LAN.

The basic Bluetooth configuration is called a Piconet. A sample Bluetooth Piconet is shown in Fig. (**2**):

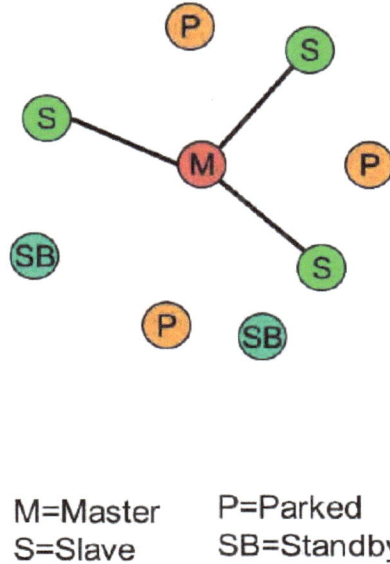

M=Master   P=Parked
S=Slave   SB=Standby

Fig. (2). Sample Bluetooth network.

In this network collection of devices is connected in an Ad hoc fashion. It contains only one master node, and other nodes are called slave nodes. Fig. **(1)** contains a Piconet having one master node and 8 slave nodes. Any communication in Piconet happens between the Master node and the Slave node. There is no direct communication possible between 2 Slave nodes. In case any two Slave nodes in the Piconet need to communicate, then communication should happen through the Master node only.

A slave node can also be set to an inactive state known as a parking state. Suppose a slave node is not at all participating in communication for a long time; then such a slave node state can be brought into a parking state to save the battery power. At a time, any number of slave nodes can be kept in a parking state. The parked slave nodes will be at inactive low power energy saving state. The collection of Piconets is known as scatternet. The sample scatternet is shown in Fig. **(3)**.

This scatternet contains 3 different piconets. Every piconet contains a single master and several slave nodes.

Fig. **(4)** shows a set of Bluetooth adaptors that are used to frame the Bluetooth network. Bluetooth can connect fixed devices as well as mobile devices. We need to connect to a desktop computer using a Bluetooth adaptor to connect to some other device, maybe a mobile device, to establish short-range communication. We have many such adaptors with different connectivity requirements.

Bluetooth Protocol Stack

Fig. (**5**) shows the Bluetooth protocol stack.

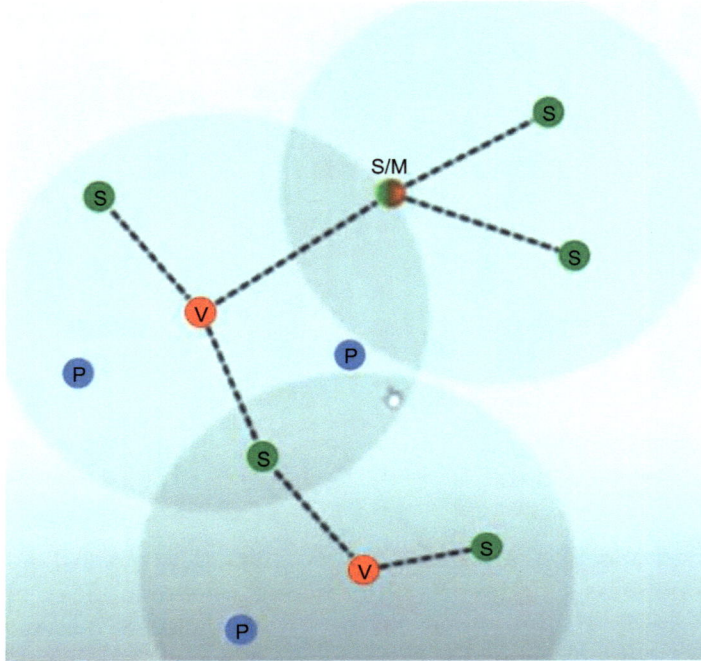

Fig. (3). Sample Scatternet.

Fig. (4). Bluetooth devices.

							Application layer
			Applications/Profiles				
Audio	Other LLC	RFcomm	Telephony	Service discovery	Control		Middleware layer
	Logical link control adaptation protocol						Data
	Link manager						link
Baseband							layer
Physical radio							Physical layer

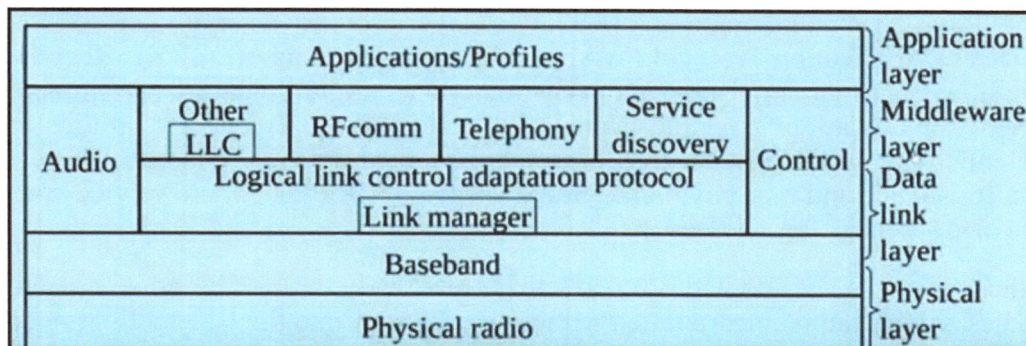

Fig. (5). Bluetooth Protocol Stack.

Here, the bottommost layer is the physical radio layer, which is responsible for defining air interface, frequency bands, frequency hopping techniques required by Bluetooth communication, the type of modulation technique required, the amount of power required to be transferred, *etc*. The baseband layer protocol is responsible for the type of addressing scheme that needs to be used, the type of data that needs to be sent or the packet frame format, and deciding which power control algorithm is required to be used to establish a connection between Bluetooth devices within the Piconet. Suppose the connection must be established between any two nodes within the Piconet; the baseband layer will take care of this connection establishment.

The Link Management layer performs the management of already established links. It also includes an authentication and encryption process to ensure the security and privacy of the connection established. Logical Link Control Adaptation Protocol (LLCAP) is the heart of the Bluetooth protocol stack. Its task is to establish the communication between the upper and lower layers of the Bluetooth protocol stack. So, it is an interface between the upper layer and lower layer of the Bluetooth protocol. The LLCAP also performs segmentation and multiplexing. Suppose the big data is to be sent from an application layer; it cannot be sent in a single stretch as Bluetooth suffers from a lower data rate. So, the data should be made into pieces known as segments before transmission. Also, when the channel is to be used by many nodes, then the multiplexing is taken care of by this layer itself.

The Service Discovery protocol is responsible for identifying various services provided by various applications as well as service providers. Service may be related to the queries including device information that can be taken care of at this protocol so that the connection gets established for any two Bluetooth devices.

The Radio Frontend Component (RFcomm) layer provides a serial interface with Wireless Application Protocol (WAP) and Object Exchange (OBEX). RFcomm works as a virtual serial port and transmits binary digital data bits. It emulates RS232 specifications over the Bluetooth physical layer. Telephony protocol or Telephony Control Protocol (TCN) is a bit-oriented protocol that specifies call control signals and mobility management procedures for telephonic services such as voice services, fax services, *etc*.

Other protocols are adopted protocols that are already defined by other standard bodies, which can be incorporated without any change into the Bluetooth protocol architecture. The protocols are PPP(Point to Point Protocol), TCP/UDP/IP, OBEX (Object Exchange Protocol), WAP(Wireless Application Protocol), *etc*.

The application layer enables a user to interact with the application [1, 2].

Bluetooth Applications

Bluetooth technology is used in many real-world applications. Following are some of the most frequently used applications:

  i. Connect to speakers and headphones:
     Using Bluetooth, we can connect to headphones and speakers to listen to music.
 ii. Wireless instant File sharing:
     With short-distance wireless communication with Bluetooth, it is possible to transfer files from one device to another.
iii. Tether a computer to a smartphone:
     Devices with Bluetooth radio can establish a connection with another when in range.

Bluetooth Security

Compared to Wi-Fi, Bluetooth is more secure, but this does not make Bluetooth completely secure. It is possible to communicate with people *via* Bluetooth even if we do not intend to do so. While communicating *via* Bluetooth, there are chances of eavesdropping, for example, while using wireless headsets. The best way to keep ourselves secure is to turn off Bluetooth when you are not making use of it and always double-check whenever you are connecting to the correct device.

Connecting to Devices via Bluetooth and Transferring Files

i. **Connecting to Speaker on a Mac:** The steps to be followed are:
  - Open your Bluetooth Settings.
  - You should see connectable devices listed with the connect button next to it, and *click connect.*
ii. **Transferring files *via* Bluetooth:** For example, to share files *via* Bluetooth between Apple devices, you can simply use the Airdrop feature. The steps to be followed are:
  - If Bluetooth is turned on in both devices, you can simply right-click (on Mac) or tap (phone/ tablet) and select Airdrop.
  - Your device should be located near Apple devices, and you can then select one to share with.
iii. **Troubleshooting Bluetooth Connection Problems:**
  - Make sure Bluetooth is turned on in both devices.
  - Turn on *discoverable mode.*
  - Power the devices off and back on.
  - Delete a device from the phone and discover it.
  - Make sure the devices you want to pair are designed to connect.
  - Make sure the two devices are in close enough proximity to each other.

ZigBee

One striking thing about the ZigBee protocol is that it functions at an extremely low data rate, and it can survive under extremely noisy conditions. ZigBee makes use of the Direct Spread Spectrum (DSS) Modulation scheme, which essentially makes it more robust to any interference and noise conditions. Therefore, this protocol is suitable for applications such as large-scale environment monitoring. As the data rate is low, it gives us the advantage of very good receiver sensitivity, which in turn supports the system with the required range. Compared to Bluetooth, ZigBee is the lowest power-consuming device, and we can get the lowest data rate from it.

The range of ZigBee can be anywhere between 10 to 100 meters. Whereas, the range of Bluetooth is anywhere between 2 to 10 meters.

ZigBee Systems Architecture

Fig. (6) shows ZigBee Systems Architecture. At the lowest level, we have a Medium Access Control (MAC) layer, which helps in accessing radio waves specified by the IEEE standard. At the top of radio waves, there is a collection of protocols called stack feature sets, which specify the network layer behavior defined by ZigBee Alliance. As per ZigBee 2007 specifications, there are two standard specifications: ZigBee and ZigBee PRO. Among these, ZigBee PRO is the dominant feature that supports energy harvesting.

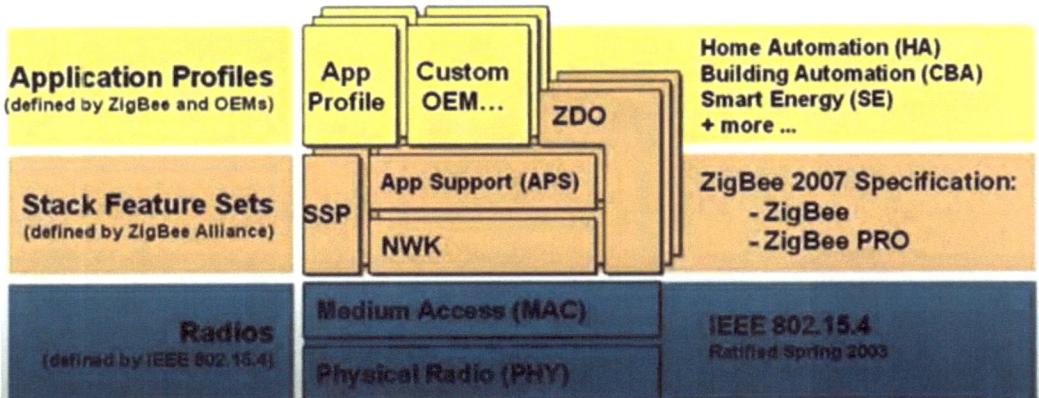

Fig. (6). ZigBee Systems Architecture.

Finally, at the highest level, there is an application layer that contains a set of guidelines known as Application Profiles defined by ZigBee to support various application use cases such as Commercial building automation, smart energy, home automation, *etc*.

ZigBee Applications

Due to the low cost, low power consumption, low latency, and low duty cycles of ZigBee (IEEE 802.15.4) protocol, it is ideal for a wide range of industrial applications as it allows the products to maximize the life of their power supply batteries. There are numerous applications of ZigBee in the real world. Some are listed below:

i. Wireless Camera System at Home: ZigBee can be used here to transmit the visitors' videos recorded at the front door by the Wireless Camera System to the dedicated monitor that is kept inside the home.

ii. ZigBee-based Automated Meter Reading System: The utility meter should read the units regularly to generate utility bills for homeowners who are connected *via* a self-forming wireless mesh network using the ZigBee network. Using these, corporate offices can monitor the regular usage of electricity, water, *etc*., remotely, eliminating the need for people visiting to note down the reading manually. Also, it helps in gathering monthly usage data that can help in automatically detecting water leakage, equipment problems, *etc*.

iii. ZigBee-enabled irrigation system: A sensor-based irrigation system can result in efficient water management. Sensors across the landscaping field can communicate with the irrigation panel about the soil moisture levels.

ZigBee versus Bluetooth

Table **1** shows the important difference between ZigBee and Bluetooth technologies.

Table 1. Differences between bluetooth and ZigBee.

-	Bluetooth	ZigBee
1.	The frequency range supported in Bluetooth varies from 2.4 GHz to 2.483 GHz.	The frequency range supported in Zigbee is mostly 2.4 GHz worldwide.
2.	There are 79 RF channels in Bluetooth.	There are sixteen RF channels in ZigBee.
3.	It uses the GFSK modulation technique.	ZigBee uses BPSK and QPSK modulation techniques like UWB.
4.	The maximum number of cell nodes in Bluetooth is 8.	ZigBee contains 65000 cell nodes.
5.	Bluetooth requires low bandwidth.	ZigBee also requires low bandwidth but more than Bluetooth.
6.	The radio signal range of Bluetooth is 2 to 10 meters.	The radio signal range of ZigBee is 10 to 100 meters.

Wireless Sensor Networks

A wireless sensor network (WSN) is an ideal technology to provide efficient and viable solutions for different applications such as environmental monitoring, agricultural monitoring, military applications, and so forth.

WSNs are applied in different areas. They have presently paved the path for body area networking, vehicle Ad hoc networking, the Internet of things, and many more based on the applications and architectures. The WSN was initially applied in military applications. Now, it is also applied in applications like building monitoring, animal monitoring and tracking, fire detection applications, landslide applications, undersea monitoring, and many more.

The typical challenges in WSNs are power management, positioning of sensors (localization), coverage of events, routing, time synchronization, security and privacy, real-time implementations, energy harvesting, and deployment.

The performance metrics of a WSN depend on various parameters. There is not one single parameter that makes an efficient WSN. The application of WSN may have a tradeoff on the parameters considered for the network. The performance metrics of the WSN are node deployment, spatial area, node density, node localization, node routing, energy of the node, radio of the sensor node, battery life of the node, security of the network, processing capability of the sensor node, computation power, sensor resolution, data rate, bandwidth, size of the mote, signal strength and many more. The other constraints influencing the sensor nodes are low power consumption, high capacity density operations, re-peaceability, being, and adaption to the surroundings.

Wireless Sensor Network (WSN) Protocol Stack

The protocols in WSN are used for communications. IEEE 802.15 series are the ones used in most of the applications. ZigBee and 6LoWPAN are the two dominant protocols used due to their low power consumption.

Fig. (7) shows the WSN protocol stack.

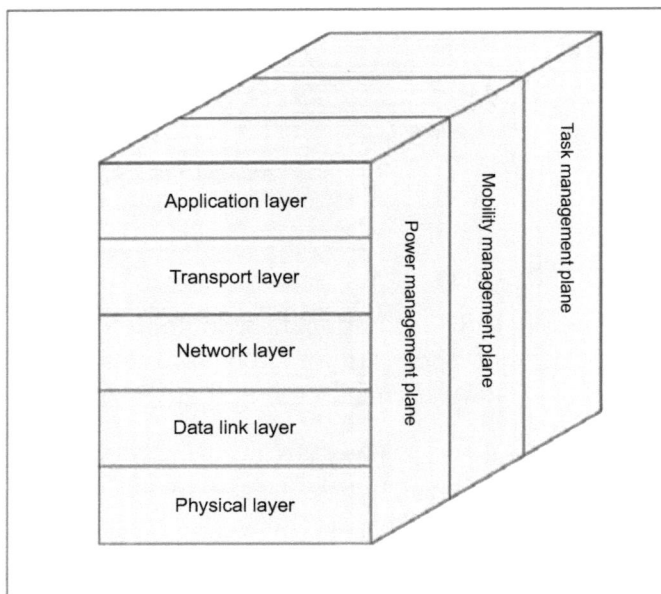

Fig. (7). Sensor Network Protocol Stack.

Wireless Image Sensor Network

A wireless image sensor network (WISN) is a network where images or visual sensor nodes are installed, which capture images/videos at regular time intervals and forward them to the remote station where images/videos are processed for decision-making.

WISN can be used in several applications such as one of such applications, which may be monitoring the growth of the crop from a remote station. In this case, the network may consist of two types of nodes: scalar nodes that sense environmental parameters such as soil moisture level, soil humidity, air temperature, air humidity, soil pH. *etc.*, and nodes that acquire the image of the crops and image sensors.

CONCLUDING REMARKS

This chapter provides an overview of WPAN in terms of various technologies used, such as ZigBee, Bluetooth, WSN, WISN, *etc*. In this chapter, the characteristics and workings of these technologies are explained.

EXERCISES

1. List and explain the categories of WPAN.
2. What do you mean by Bluetooth network? Explain.
3. With a neat diagram, explain the Bluetooth protocol stack.
4. What do you mean by ZigBee network? Explain.
5. List the differences between Bluetooth and ZigBee networks.
6. With a neat diagram, explain the WSN Protocol stack.
7. What do you mean by WISN? Explain.

REFERENCES

[1]   M. Miller, "The internet of things: How smart tvs, smart cars, smart homes and smart cities are changing the world", 2015.

[2]   E. Sazonov, and M.R. Neuman, "Wearable sensors: fundamentals, implementation, and applications", In: Academic Press/Elsevier, 2014.

CHAPTER 6

Wireless Sensor Networks

Abstract: A Wireless Sensor Network (WSN) is a category Network. As the name suggests, the nodes are capable of sensing. Sensing is a physical phenomenon that occurs around them. Sensor nodes of WSN can sense humidity, pressure, temperature, light, sound, vibration, color, *etc*. Sensor nodes have one main component called a sensor, and these sensor nodes collectively make a network known as WSN. WSN is one of the very popular networks due to diverse types of applications, such as tracking objects, healthcare, agriculture, space applications, and so on. WSN is a key formation of the Internet of Things (IoT). IoT and WSN have been very important components for building smart cities in recent years in our country as well as across the globe. In this chapter, the need for WSN, the building block of WSN, the next design of WSN, the application of WSN, *etc*., are discussed.

Keywords: WSN, Sensors, WSN architecture, WSN applications.

INTRODUCTION

WSN is a collection of different sensors; these sensors are densely deployed and can capture the variety of physical phenomena occurring around them. Sensor nodes can be equipped with various types of sensors. Sensor nodes can collaborate and measure sound, light, temperature, *etc*., from surrounding environments. This sensed data can then be converted to digital signals and then processed to reveal the properties of the phenomenon.

Usually, sensor nodes are capable of capturing data from short distances through radio transmission range; however, by using relay nodes or intermediate nodes in WSN, it is possible to communicate nodes that exist from long distances. So, what we essentially see here is similar to what we observed in the case of an Ad doc network or multi-hop kind of architecture. Basically sensor network is used to sense data from short-range distances using a wireless medium, and by using multi-hop architecture, they transmit the data to the destination node, which is far apart. The destination node in WSN is termed a sink node or base station. There is a difference between the sink node and the base station. The sink node is necessarily a sensor node, whereas the base station may not be a sensor node. For example, there can be a computer at the sink node that will be stored in that computing device.

Why do we need a Sensor Network? What is the Difference between a Sensor and a WSN?

Individual sensor nodes embedded with sensors can sense the phenomena locally in a fixed location, whereas in WSN, it is possible to deploy multiple such sensor nodes over a large distance, which can even communicate with each other to get an idea about what is happening in such a larger area. So basically, to cover bigger areas, WSN becomes useful. WSN is also very useful when someone wants to observe or monitor such areas remotely in an unmanned fashion to find out what is happening in that larger area. Typical WSN is as shown below in Fig. (1).

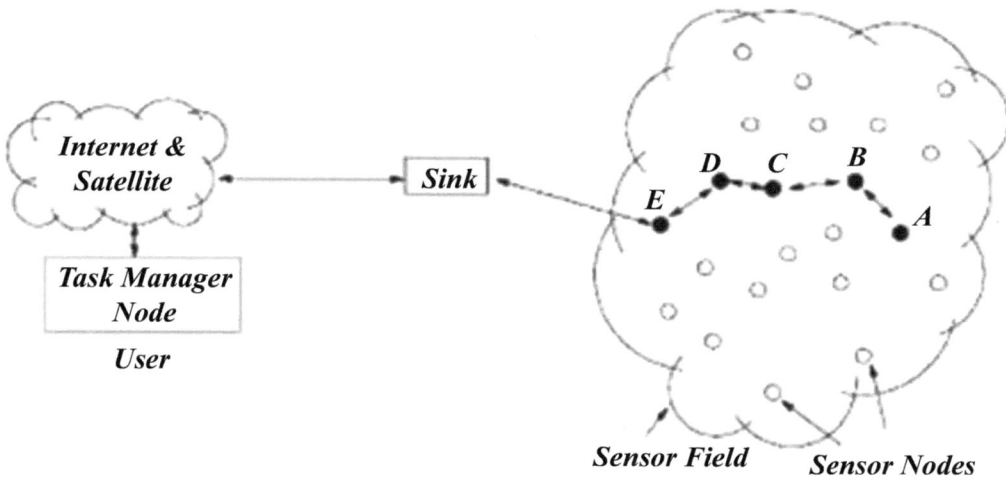

Fig. (1). Typical WSN.

Classification of WSN

WSN is broadly classified into two types: Stationary and Mobile.

a. **Stationary WSN:** This is a classical form of sensor network. In stationary WSNs, nodes in the network are fixed. None of the nodes is mobile.

b. **Mobile WSN:** In Mobile WSN, at least one or all the sensor nodes are mobile. Here, some of the nodes or all nodes would move. Mobile WSN is used in plenty of applications. This WSN is found mostly in oceans, terrestrial environments (Sensors fitted to vehicles), aerial sensor networks, or UAVs (Unmanned Aerial Vehicles).

Basic Architecture of WSN

A typical sensor node in WSN can communicate with each other through radio signals. Each sensor node in WSN is capable of sensing using its sensing unit, processing using its processing unit, and communicating using a transceiver unit. Sensor nodes in WSN have limited processing speed, limited storage capacity, and limited bandwidth. In addition to 4 units, application-dependent units are also present in WSN. This means whatever we have seen in a mini computer is available in sensor networks such as input units or sensing units, communication facilities, processing units, and output units. Fig. (**2**) shows the basic architecture of WSN.

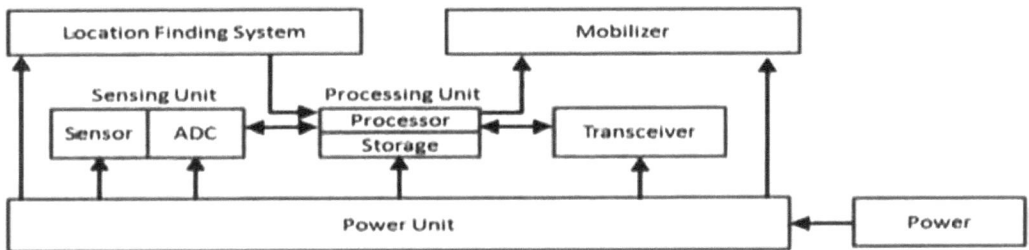

Fig. (2). Basic architecture of WSN.

Constraints on the Sensor Nodes in WSN

The following shows the constraints on typical sensor nodes in WSN:

a. *Be small in size:* Typically, less than a cubic centimeter.
b. *Consume less energy:* Nodes in WSN consume very low energy.
c. *Operate in an unattended manner:* Nodes in WSN are designed to operate in an unattended manner in a highly dense area.
d. *Low cost:* Sensor nodes are available at low production costs. Nodes can also be fabricated at low cost; hence, if the node is damaged for one or another reason or drains out of energy, then they can be dispensable.
e. *Be autonomous:* Sensor nodes, once deployed, operate autonomously in any area without human intervention.
f. *Be adaptive to the environment:* If there is a change in the environment, then nodes should be in a position to recognize that change accordingly.

Challenges to be Faced in Building Sensor Networks

For any typical application, WSN needs to be designed and implemented. Some of the common challenges to be faced in building a sensor network are listed below:

a. *Scalability:* If we increase the number of nodes in the sensor network, then how does the throughput perform? If 'n' represents the number of nodes in the network, then throughput reduces at the rate of $1/\sqrt{n}$. For instance, if we increase the number of nodes from 10 to 20, then throughput reduces drastically, which is a serious drawback of WSN. Suppose we need to deploy a large number of nodes in the network; how do we handle this?

b. *Quality of Service(QoS):* QoS means offering guaranteed service with an adequate amount of bandwidth, delay, and jitter. Offering a guarantee in terms of required bandwidth, required delay, and required jitter is the major necessity of any application. But guaranteed QoS parameters are very difficult to achieve due to some of the characteristics of WSN, such as noise, limited bandwidth, unpredictable changes in RF channel characteristics, and the environment in which WSN is deployed, which is quite chaotic.

c. *Energy efficiency:* Nodes have limited battery power. The nodes are not only responsible for their task; instead, they need to rely on other nodes for data transmission, so efficient handling of energy is very challenging.

d. Security: As this network works with an open medium like other wireless networks, nodes are more prone to attacks such as denial of service, eavesdropping, interference, *etc.* This makes WSNs vulnerable to many types of attacks, so providing security is a very important concern in these networks.

Sensor Networks Deployment

Sensor networks consist of sensor nodes, which is one of the fundamental components of sensor network deployment. Sensor nodes consist of sensors. For a particular application, while deploying WSN, it is required to identify the type of sensor to be used with sensor nodes. Sensor networks can be used in a wide range of applications. While deploying the WSN, the fundamental configuration needs to be known.

Two of the important problems that need to be known while deploying are problems of coverage and problems of placement.

a. *Problem of coverage:* It is basically deployment. Sensor nodes first need to be procured and then need to be deployed in a particular area. For deployment, every part is under the sensing range. The main objective of the problem is to find out whether every point in the targeted or interested field is within the sensing range of the deployed sensors [1].

b. *Coverage Area:* There are 2 types of modes in which the sensor operates: Static mode and Mobile mode. The coverage problem of the static sensor node is different from the coverage problem of the mobile sensor node. Coverage problem means an area of interest. The area of interest must be covered

satisfactorily. At least one sensor node should be under the surveillance of the area of interest.
c. *Connectivity:* There must be connectivity between the nodes that are about to communicate with each other so that the data sent can eventually reach the destination. Coverage and connectivity are related to each other. This means if the coverage is ensured, then connectivity will also be ensured.

To Understand more about the Coverage and Connectivity

Let us understand some of the basic definitions. When we talk about sensor nodes, in terms of ranges, the wireless sensor has two ranges: sensing range and transmission range. The sensing range is nothing but how far the node can sense. Transmission range is nothing but how far the sensed data gets transmitted to some other node or sink node in the network.

Let us denote the sensing range by r_s and the transmission range by r_t. Zhang and Hou [2] proved that if the communication range r_t is twice the sensing range r_s, then the coverage implies connectivity. Now, to say that there is a coverage area, the following condition must be satisfied:

Transmission range $>= 2 *$ sensing range

i.e., $r_t >= * r_s$

The above condition determines the relationship between coverage and connectivity. Most sensors satisfy the above conditions. This means coverage is ensured. Coverage is the main issue in sensor networks. The above condition also says that coverage implies connectivity. So we need not have to worry about the connectivity problem once the coverage is satisfied. Connectivity is automatically taken care of when we ensure the coverage.

The coverage problem talks about determining how well the sensing field is tracked by the sensors. In the case of static sensors, the coverage area is determined based on where exactly the sensors get deployed. But, in the case of mobile sensors, how to determine the trajectory of mobile sensors?

The purpose of deploying a wireless sensor node is to collect relevant data for processing. So, WSN will sense the data from the particular area and then rely on that data to the base station for further processing. As per the application, some events may be happening, so the sensor nodes will detect those events, sense them, and then relay that information to the base station or sink node. The application may be either event-driven or inventory-based in event-driven applications, such as sensing vital information from patients during an emergency.

In the case of on-demand, a query is sent to the sensor node, and a reply is received from the node. An example of an on-demand application is the inventory control system. While deploying the WSN, care must be taken to select a minimum number of sensors and increase the network lifetime. So, for a specific application, if we need to deploy WSN, we need to identify the adequate number of sensors and then sense the information by event-driven method or on-demand method.

Coverage algorithms are classified into the following three categories:

a. *Centralized:* Here, the data is collected centrally, and the global map of the WSN is obtained from a central point.
b. *Distributed:* Here, the nodes compute their position by communicating with their neighbors only.
c. *Localized:* These are special types of distributed algorithms in which only a subset of nodes in WSN participate in sensing, communicating, and computing.

There are different methods for deploying sensor nodes:

a. *Deterministic:* In this method of deployment, the sensor node position is predetermined. For example, if there are a set of sensor nodes, say x, y, and z, then the position of these nodes in the region of interest is known in advance.
b. *Random:* This deployment is airborne means sensors are deployed by using aircraft or helicopters. Here, the nodes are spread across under area in which sensing is going to happen. The nodes, once spread, fall on the ground, and they sense the required information from that location and send it to the base station.

Coverage Problem in Static WSN

Coverage problem in static WSN is classified into the following 3 categories:

a. *Area Coverage:* Area coverage means energy-efficient random coverage, wherein it is required to cover every area in the particular region of interest. Here, some kind of random coverage should be ensured, which means each point in that area needs to be covered. It has been proved that the communication range rt is two times the sensing range rs, and then the coverage implies connectivity. One of the important observations is that an area is completely covered if there are at least two disks that intersect and all crossings are covered, which means a circle in 2D or a sphere in 3D around a particular sensor. One unit of this disk is nothing but one radius of this particular disk. Based on this, the authors proposed a distributed and localized algorithm called the optimal geographical density control algorithm [2]. Here, the surroundings are nothing but one unit or area of the particular disk.

b. *Point Coverage:* In point coverage, we have a set of points instead of an area. The area is nothing but a set of infinite points, whereas, in point coverage, we deal with a set of points in a particular area. In this case, sensor nodes are deployed in such a way that those points of interest are covered by at least one sensor node. That means at least one sensor node should be in a position to sense that particular point. Here, at least one sensor node must be in a position to cover the point. Again, under this point coverage, we have 2 categories, *i.e.,* Deterministic point coverage and Random point coverage.

c. *Barrier Coverage:* In the barrier coverage, there will be some kind of barrier; for example, in the port, there may be some high wall, and outside the wall, there can be a typical water body surrounding it. Another real-time example could be the border between the two different countries, *i.e.,* the international border. In this case, we may want to have some sort of monitoring happening in such a way that if any person crosses the border will be recorded by the WSN. This means at the border, on both sides, several sensors are deployed in such a way that there is no person who can come without being detected by at least one sensor in that area.

As shown in Fig. (**3**), the person who is crossing the border (represented in red arrow) may be detected by either the immediate left sensor or right sensor as both are in the same range or area. The blue arrow shows there is no crossing of the border, so when the person may move near the border, the sensor detects it. Barrier coverage can be categorized into one-barrier coverage, two-barrier coverage, k coverage, *etc.*, based on how many sensors can detect the crossing of the border. Under one-barrier coverage, one sensor node can detect the crossing of the border; in two-barrier coverage, at least two sensor nodes can detect the crossing of the border. Similarly, in k-barrier coverage, at least k sensor nodes can detect the crossing of the border.

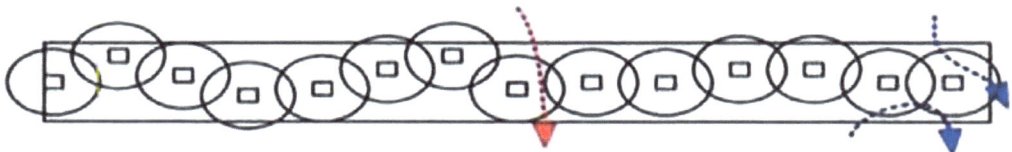

Fig. (3). Barrier Coverage Scenario.

The barrier coverage model can be of two types based on how strong the coverage is. If somebody can cross the border without even being detected by a single sensor, then it is called weak area coverage. If the person crossing the border is detected by at least one sensor node deployed at the border, then it is called strong area coverage. Two types of barrier coverage models are shown in Fig. (**4**).

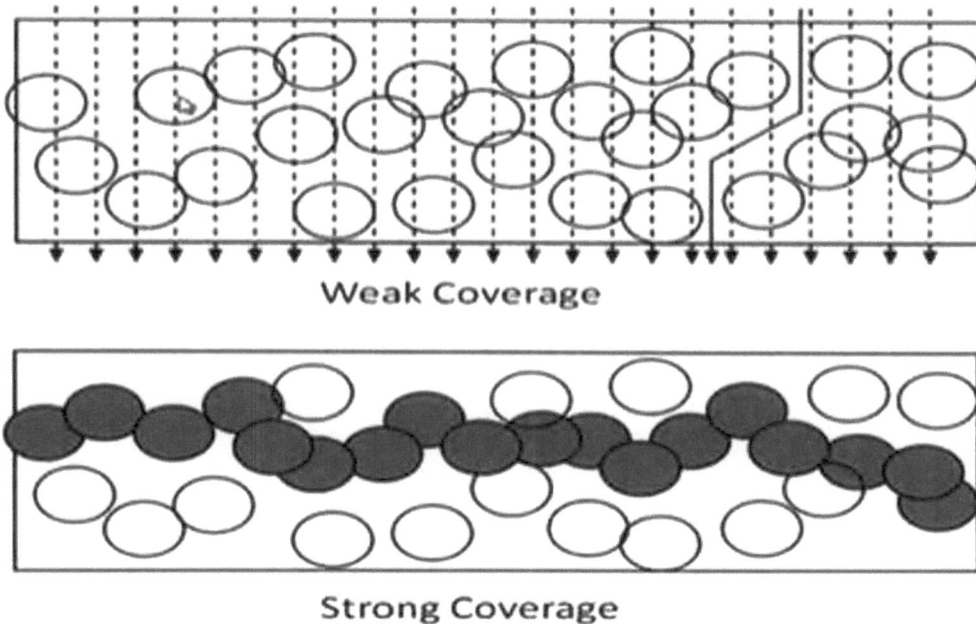

Weak Coverage

Strong Coverage

Fig. (4). Barrier Coverage Model Types.

The area coverage problem concerning WSN is explained by Zhang and Hou [1] as given below:

Area coverage problems in WSNs have been widely studied for many years, wherein the main objective of the study is to cover or monitor an area sometimes referred to as region R. A region R is covered only if there are crossings in that region R and every such crossing in region R is covered [3].

Applications of WSN

WSN can be used in plenty of applications such as precision agriculture, forest fire detection, smart metering, healthcare monitoring, and so on.

a. *Applications of WSN in Healthcare:* One of the important applications of WSN is in healthcare. A lot of research has been done and is ongoing in this area. As shown in Fig. (**5**), WBAN (Wireless Body Area Networks) is a short-range wireless network of multiple wearable computing devices placed over or near or implanted inside the human body:

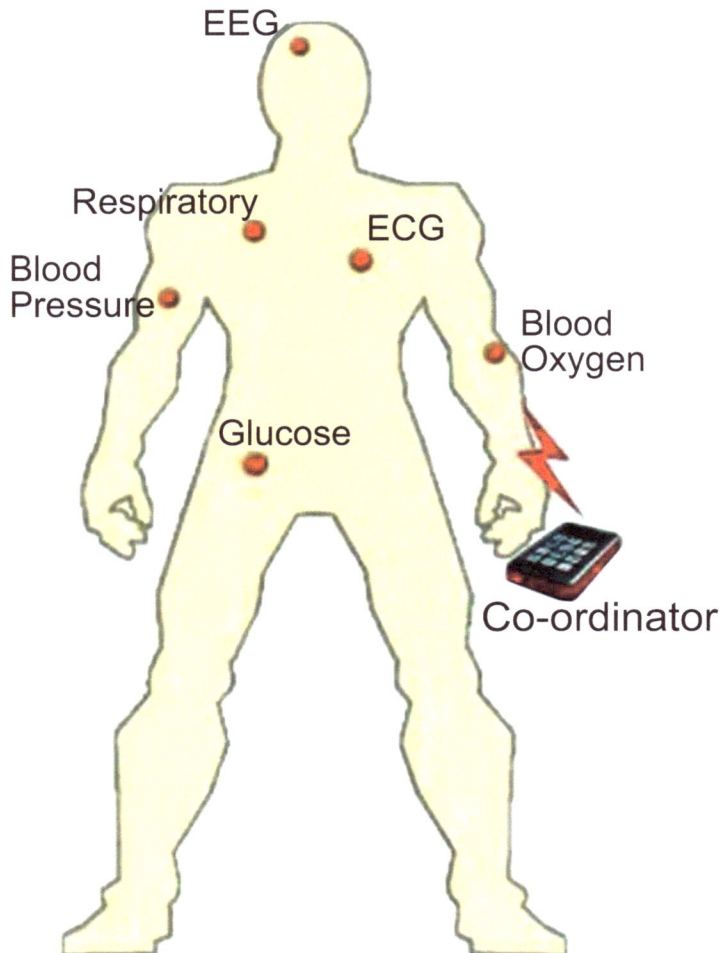

Fig. (5). Wireless Body Area Network.

These devices have built-in sensors that are responsible for sensing vital information such as blood pressure, temperature, heart rate, respiration, electrocardiogram, *etc.*, of the person. These devices are either placed inside the body or on the surface of the body in a fixed position. The information sensed by the sensors is then forwarded to the coordinator node, *i.e.*, either a PDA (Personal

Digital Assistant) or smartphone. The coordinator analyzes the received data, takes an appropriate decision, and forwards data along with decision information related to the condition of the human body. The applications of WBAN are numerous, such as healthcare, fitness, telemedicine, personal information sharing, sports training, continuous monitoring in emergencies, *etc*. Fig. (**6**) shows the BAN and its components.

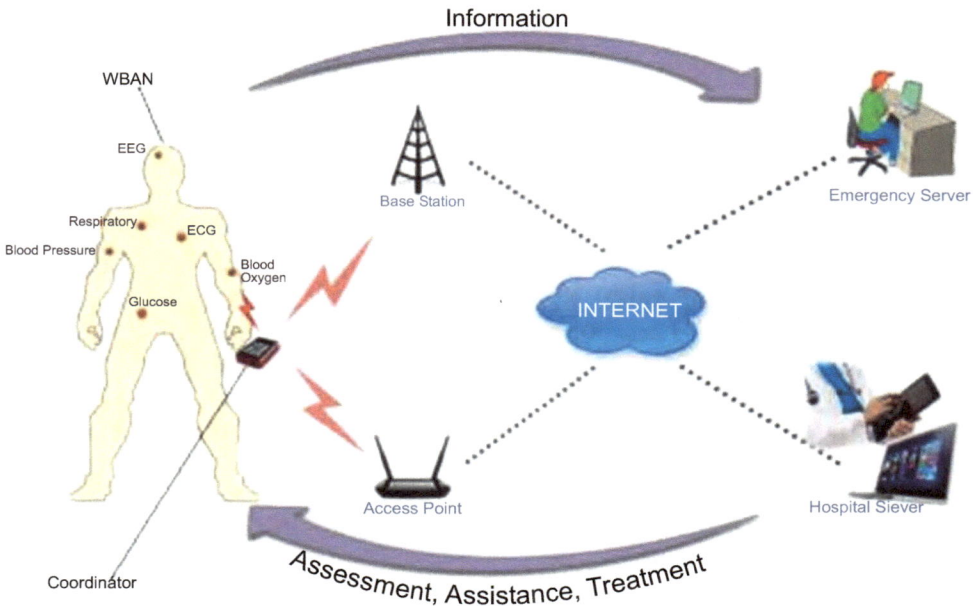

Fig. (6). WBAN components.

WBAN is an extension of the Wide Area Network. If we talk about WBAN in the context of IoT, these wearable devices belong to things in the Internet of Things. WBANs can be further classified into In-body communications, Off-body communications, and On-body communications, depending on how these things/sensors are placed in specific applications. In the case of in-body, sensors are placed inside the body to sense vital information from the body. Similarly, in the case of off-body communications, sensors are placed to collect the environmental conditions, such as the presence of heat, fire, lighting, smoke, *etc*., during the disaster recovery process.

Many studies have been published that discuss these issues using an automated electronic triage telemedicine system, in which vital sign sensors are implanted in human bodies to measure vital sign parameters continuously. In addition, medical team members use a Clinical Decision Support System (CDSS) to interpret observed facts to determine the casualties' current clinical status. Some works [4 - 6] are developed for triaging the casualty in the disaster scenario.

Sensors are an essential component of IoT devices. Sensors can measure patient vital parameters such as body temperature, blood pressure, pulse rate, heart rate, glucose levels, and more. These sensors can be integrated into wearable devices, medical equipment, and even inside the human body. Using this technology, doctors can remotely monitor the patient's vital parameters at regular intervals [7, 8].

a. *Applications of WSN in Precision Agriculture:* Precision agriculture resulted from the advancement in WSNs and soft computing techniques. This model helps to re-organize the entire farming system with low input, high efficiency, and sustainable farming. As a branch of soft computing techniques, machine learning has been widely used in various applications for classification tasks. WSNs are the driving force behind precision agriculture. Together, these technologies are contributing to building various decision support systems that help farmers to know the conditions of soil, crop, and other environmental factors and make important decisions like when to start sowing, spray pesticides and herbicides, apply fertilizers, and so on. This has resulted in increased crop production and yield.

The WSN was implemented in a field at the Agricultural Research Institute, Hyderabad, as shown in Fig. (**7**).

In several studies [9, 10], the design and development of new sensing modules were reported and compared with commercially available sensing modes. Authors believe that commercially available nodes, such as Mica2, TelosB, *etc.*, are expensive and sometimes not suitable for long-range communication. Moreover, applications like precision agriculture and environmental monitoring applications require sensing modules in large numbers for more precise data collection so that timely decisions can be taken. As a result, using commercially available sensing nodes makes the implementation cost too high, which may not be feasible. Therefore, they report on developing new sensing modules. They have used the wireless module MRF24J40 and microprocessor STM32L152. The modules were programmed using Keil-C. The performance of the new sensing module was compared with the commercially available module using read-range, PER, RSSI, and LQI parameters. The result showed that the new sensing modules have full potential for applications in precision agriculture. The new implementation had a read range (over 150m), RSSI (bigger than -v80dBm), LQI (bigger than 108), and PRR (over 99%) in the range between 0 and 150. Sensing nodes sense the parameters, and the gateway node is a system that receives the data from other sensory data, and the controller controls the array of nodes [9, 10]. Fig. (**8**) shows the fabricated sensor node.

Fig. (7). WSN Deployment Site.

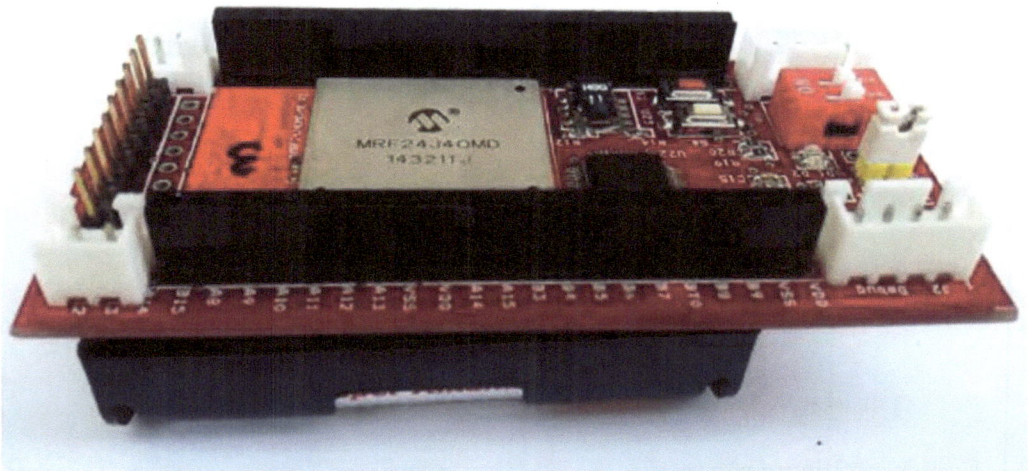

Fig. (8). Fabricated module of the wireless sensing node.

More recent literature on IoT applications is available [11, 12], which includes integration of WSN with IoT for real-world applications.

CONCLUDING REMARKS

This chapter provides the basics of wireless sensor networks, classification of WSN, architecture, coverage, applications, *etc.*

EXERCISES

1. Mention the characteristics of WSN.
2. How does coverage imply connectivity in WSN? Justify.
3. Distinguish between WSN and Sensor.
4. What do you mean by Barrier coverage concerning WSN?
5. Illustrate Area coverage problems concerning Sensor networks.
6. How does WSN help in Healthcare applications?

REFERENCES

[1]   Available from: https://ieeexplore.ieee.org/stamp/stamp.jsp?tp=&arnumber=7955741

[2]   H. Zhang, and J. Hou, "Maintaining sensing coverage and connectivity in large sensor networks", *International Journal of Ad Hoc & Sensor Wireless Networks,* vol. 1, no. 1-2, pp. 89-124, 2005. [http://dx.doi.org/10.1201/9780203323687.ch28]

[3]   Yu Wang, Xiang-Yang Li, and Qian Zhang, "Efficient algorithms for the p-self-protection problem in static wireless sensor networks", *IEEE Transactions On Parallel And Distributed Systems,* vol. 19, no. 10, pp. 1234-1245, 2008.

[4]   D.B. Arbia, M.M. Alam, R. Attia, and E.B. Hamida, "A novel multi-hop body-to-body routing protocol for disaster and emergency networks", *International Conference on Wireless Networks and Mobile Communications (WINCOM),* pp. 246-252, 2016. [http://dx.doi.org/10.1109/WINCOM.2016.7777222]

[5]   K. Sakanushi, T. Hieda, T. Shiraishi, Y. Ode, Y. Takeuchi, M. Imai, T. Higashinoz, and H. Tanaka, "Electronic triage system: Casualties monitoring system in the disaster scene", In: *IEEE Explorer,* 2011, pp. 317-322.

[6]   O.H. Salman, M.F.A. Rasid, M.I. Saripan, and S.K. Subramaniam, "Multi-sources data fusion framework for remote triage prioritization in telehealth", *J. Med. Syst.,* vol. 38, no. 9, p. 103, 2014. [http //dx.doi.org/10.1007/s10916-014-0103-4] [PMID: 25047520]

[7]   C. Li, J. Wang, S. Wang, and Y. Zhang, "A review of IoT applications in healthcare", In: *Neurocomputing* Elsevier, 2024.

[8]   T. Gao, T. Massey, L. Selavo, D. Crawford, B. Chen, K. Lorincz, V. Shnayder, L. Hauenstein, F. Dabiri, J. Jeng, A. Chanmugam, D. White, M. Sarrafzadeh, and M. Welsh, "The advanced health and disaster aid network: a light-weight wireless medical system for triage", *IEEE Trans. Biomed. Circuits Syst.,* vol. 1, no. 3, pp. 203-216, 2007. [http://dx.doi.org/10.1109/TBCAS.2007.910901] [PMID: 23852414]

[9]   F. Balducci, D. Impedovo, and G. Pirlo, "Machine learning applications on agricultural datasets for smart farm enhancement", *Machines,* vol. 6, no. 3, p. 38, 2018. [http://dx.doi.org/10.3390/machines6030038]

[10]   P. Tan Lam, T. Quang Le, N. Nguyen Le, and S. Dat Nguyen, "Wireless sensing modules for rural

monitoring and precision agriculture applications", *Journal of Information and Telecommunication,* vol. 2, no. 1, pp. 107-123, 2018.
[http://dx.doi.org/10.1080/24751839.2017.1390653]

[11]   K. Bajaj, B. Sharma, and R. Singh, "Integration of wsn with iot applications: A vision, architecture, and future challenge", *Springer Nature,* 2020.

[12]   N. Mowla, N. Mowla, A.F.M. Shahen Shah, and Khaled M. Rabie, "Internet of things and wireless sensor networks for smart agriculture applications: A survey", In: *IEEE Access*, 2023, pp. 145813-145852.

CHAPTER 7

Fundamentals of 5G Networks

Abstract: 5G is one of the emerging cellular networks, which is the successor of the 4G cellular network. Even though 5G technology development started in the year 2010, its deployment started in the year 2019. In 2020, 5G was deployed in a full-fledged manner. 5G supports several applications, such as enhanced broadband, smart cities, vehicle-to-vehicle connectivity, *etc*. It uses one of the new technologies, MIMO. 5G and IoT are powerful combinations for connectivity. 5G technology has marked a transformative era in the realm of connectivity, promising speed, low latency, and enhanced network capability. The proliferation of IoT devices on 5G presents security challenges, as many devices lack security features.

Keywords: 4G, 5G, IoT, LTE, Massive MIMO, MIMO, OFDM.

INTRODUCTION

Fifth-generation wireless communication is very different from its earlier generations. In the case of earlier generations, it was more about data rates and spectral efficiency, whereas in 5G, millions of technologies must come together in terms of various layers, from the physical layer to the access layer and the network layer. This generation was deployed in 2020, so 5G is also known as IMT 2020. In 2015, the International Telecommunication Union (ITU) established a focus group IMT. Its main task is to analyze how emerging 5G technology will interact with the future network. The main aim of ITU is to identify the KPI(Key Performance Identifier) requirements of the current generation. The study that was conducted covered high-level network architecture, end-to-end QoS framework, emerging network technologies, mobile front-haul and back-haul, and network softwarization. 5G gives all that is given by 4G. In addition to this, it gives something even better. 5G was deployed in almost all places of the world in 2020. This is the era of the Internet of Things [1, 2].

The requirement of 4G in terms of data rate was only up to 10Mbps, but for 5G, it is up to 100Mbps. The mobility of 4G (LTE advanced) is supposed to serve 350km per hour, and the requirement of 5G is 500km per hour, mainly for bullet trains. The latency requirement of 5G is 1 msec. Another important concern about

5G is that it must support 1 million devices per square kilometer. Here, the devices are nothing but IoT devices.

To meet the above requirements, ITU has made certain use cases. Some of the important use cases are enhanced broadband, scalability, tactile Internet, high-speed mobility, vehicle-to-vehicle communication, smart cities, rural connectivity automation, *etc.*

5G Internet

5 key characteristics of 5G, which make it better than 4G, are:

  i. Better or optimized signals
 ii. Efficient transmission
iii. Green signaling
 iv. Low latency design
  v. Larger bandwidth

Better Signals

The base station serves multiple users at the same time. For this, the spectrum has to be divided using OFDM. Here, OFDM is the advanced version of FDM. OFDM is the heart of 4G as well as 5G. The difference is that in 4G, the smallest division we can make in the spectrum is up to 15kHertz. But there is no such division in 5G; that is, we can have spectrum division of up to 120kHz. Not only that, we can mix and match. 5G waveforms are optimized much better than 4G. So, 5G OFDM is much more advanced than 4G.

Efficient Transmission

Green Signaling

Look at the KPI(Key Performance Indicator) based on the energy efficiency of the network. For efficient transmission, all the required KPIs are achieved in this type of network.

Low Latency Design

It is nothing but a faster response. Because of this, we can play online games, and we can implement control systems on a 5G network. This completely depends on how the signaling happens, and waveforms are transferred.

Larger Bandwidth

5G systems operate with a larger bandwidth than the 4G systems. For this, the requirement is to use the new set of frequencies, especially the millimeter range of frequencies. Because of this characteristic, it is possible to get a high range of throughput from the 5G networks.

5G Working

How does OFDM make 5G functional?

It serves multiple users so that they can operate with a reasonably high data rate. Given a base station and a bandwidth/spectrum, how can the base station serve or transmit data to multiple users? The basic idea here is to divide the spectrum into multiple smaller spectrums and use each of these spectrums to serve multiple users. Once these spectrums have been used for the list of users, then again provide the spectrum to another set of users. This is called FDM. OFDM is the smart way of achieving FDM. OFDM is the smart way of implementing the frequency division function. Fig. (1) shows the division of the frequency spectrum for multiple users:

Divide the spectrum!

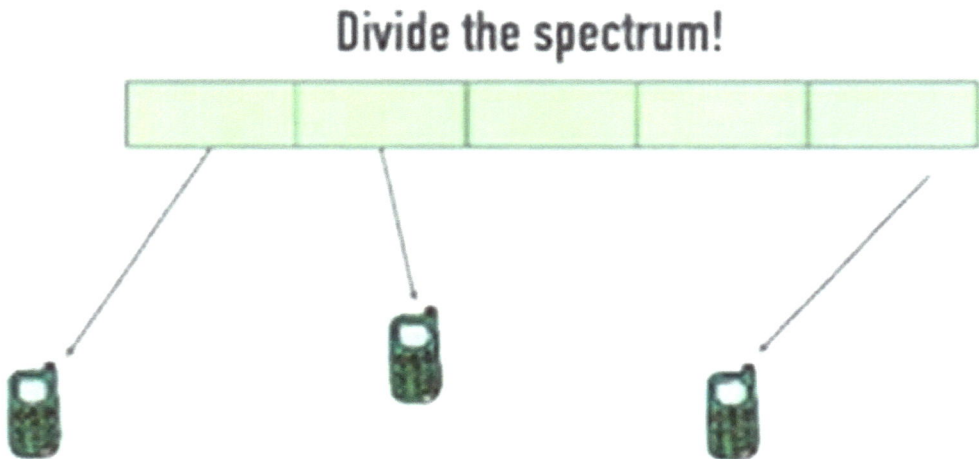

Fig. (1). Dividing frequency spectrum for multiple users using OFDM.

OFDM has been used earlier in 4G networks as well as Wi-Fi. OFDM is an advanced version of FDM. OFDM is the main core or heart of 4G as well as 5G. How does OFDM in 5G differ from 4G? In 4G, the smallest spectrum that we can make for each user is 15KHZ, whereas 5G provides multiple such options. With 5G OFDM, it is possible to make a frequency spectrum of variable sizes such as

15KHZ, 30KHZ, 120KHZ, and 240KHZ. Not only that, we can also mix and match, which is not available in 4G. So, the 5G OFDM is much more advanced than the 4G OFDM. With 5G, it is possible to pack users in a much more efficient manner. So, 5G OFDM is a much more advanced version of 4G.

MIMO (Multiple Input Multiple Output) Technology

In 4G, when the signal is transmitted through the available antenna (maybe one/two antennas), it goes all around. Here, the base station transmits the signal all around, and the hope is that there is enough power to decode the signal and run the applications. Due to this, power or energy gets wasted. So, energy must not be wasted unnecessarily. So, in 5G, care is taken while transmitting the signal. *i.e.,* instead of transmitting the signal wherever it is not necessary and wasting a lot of power, the signal is transmitted wherever it is necessary so that the user equipment will have enough power to receive the signal. The idea here is not to transmit the signal wherever it is not necessary. Fig. (**2**) shows the transmission of a signal to the required user. To do this, the technique used is to have targeted views. It focuses on a particular view and then transmits the signal. Due to this, we can serve the users efficiently with less energy. How to have targeted views? The solution is to have a massive MIMO.

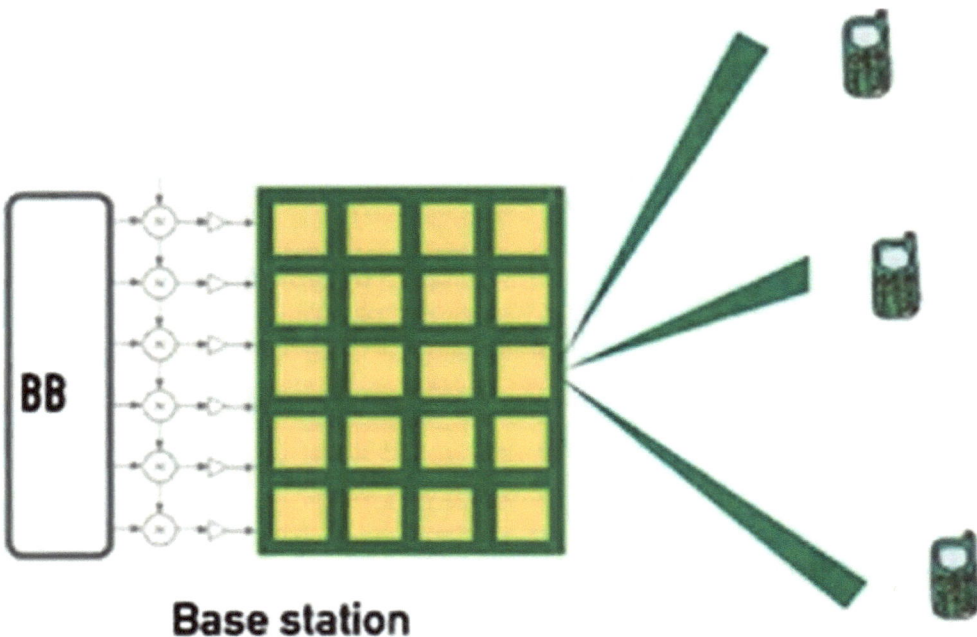

Base station

Fig. (2). Transmission of signal to the required user in 5G.

In massive MIMO, instead of transmitting the signal over a large antenna, it should be transmitted through several smaller antennas, as shown in Fig. (3). The idea here is whenever the signal needs to be transmitted, it should not be transmitted everywhere, resulting in the loss of power unnecessarily. Now consider Shannon's formula, which relates the signal-to-noise ratio to the channel capacity. Here, the channel capacity (C) is nothing but C=NWlog(1+SNR), where 'N' corresponds to the number of antennas that we have. The signal-to-noise ratio is the power that we receive at the receiver. The capacity can improve the amount of data that can be pumped.

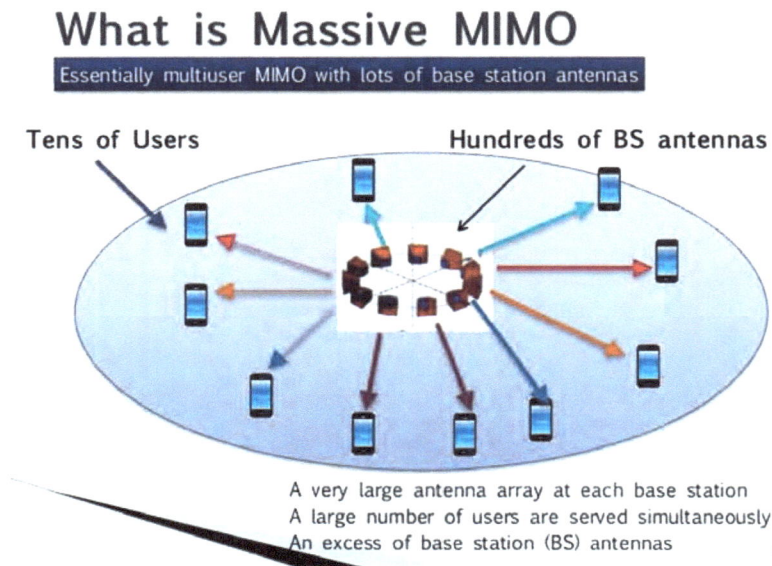

What is Massive MIMO
Essentially multiuser MIMO with lots of base station antennas

Tens of Users   Hundreds of BS antennas

A very large antenna array at each base station
A large number of users are served simultaneously
An excess of base station (BS) antennas

Fig. (3). 5G: Massive MIMO.

OFDM is used together with MIMO techniques to further increase the data rates [3]. Hence, it can be argued that OFDM is also a strong candidate for the 5G systems.

The massive MIMO helps in several ways:

 i. It increases the capacity.
ii. It focuses the energy on the users to whom we want to send the signal rather than transmitting it all around.

As per Shannon's formula, one way to increase the channel capacity is to use a larger 'N' or increase the number of antennas, and the other way is by increasing the 'W' or the bandwidth of the system. If we look at LTE, the bandwidth that the single carrier can support is 20MHz.

In 5G, the system designers thought of increasing the bandwidth to more than 20GHz. So, they introduced MM (Millimeter) wave bands. MM wave bands are nothing but frequency bands that are above 20GHz. The advantage is that in the MM wave band, a large amount of bandwidth is available; that is, we can get a large amount of bandwidth that will be available for our cellular operation. In some countries, few GHz frequency bandwidth is available. This, in turn, increases the data rate.

As the signal frequency increases, signal propagation becomes more and more difficult. The loss of the channel increases as we increase the frequency. This means that the loss of the channel that we get for 20GHz is much higher than the loss that we get for 700MHz or 400MHz. To solve this problem in MM wave bands, Phased Arrays are used. MM wave phased arrays are especially used in radar applications. This MM wave band has led to more innovation in 5G in terms of devices, phased arrays, and developing technologies in beam theorem and beam management.

So, more and more innovation is happening in 5G Technology since its introduction a decade ago. The current 5G specification has a very good framework and is flexible, so we can do a lot of things with the 5G specifications, such as we can add, configure, and make the system much better. Also, a lot of new technologies are possible with this framework, such as full duplex, where we can simultaneously transmit and receive data, Vehicle-to-Vehicle technology, *etc.*

In India, the Government is giving a lot of importance to this 5G network by helping researchers and academic institutes to improve the existing features of 5G technology. The entire working of the 5G network is known only when we start working with its features. So far, a bunch of institutes have gone to the government and started building what is known as the 5G Testbed. The goal of the 5G Testbed is to build an end-to-end system. 5G Testbed is funded by the Department of Telecommunications.

5G Use Cases

Use cases are very important for businesses' sense and deployment of any technology. Several use cases were in mind during the deployment of 5G by ITU (International Telecommunication Union). 5G should support one million devices per square kilometer, which means that these many devices of IoT should be supported by 5G. The following are some important use cases:

(i). Enhanced Broadband: To make cellular systems act like mobile Wi-Fi. Essentially, 5G is used to increase the broadband across the devices such as web cameras,and surveillance cameras available across the city to be connected *via* this network.

(ii). Ultra Dense: 4G does not support a huge number of connections in certain situations, for example, while watching a cricket match, the throughput goes down drastically. As LTE was not designed to take so many users at the same time, so 5G is designed to take care of this.

(iii). Vehicle to Vehicle connectivity: This is required for self-driving cars.

5G and IoT Integration

IoT is creating a powerful alliance that has the potential to redefine how the devices communicate, share data, and contribute to a seamlessly connected world. The technical foundations of 5G and IoT integration rest upon the pillars of high-speed data transfer, low latency, and the adaptability afforded by network slicing. The fusion of 5G and the IoT is reshaping the urban landscape, giving rise to the concept of smart cities characterized by interconnected and intelligent infrastructure.

In the realm of smart cities, 5G's high-speed data transfer capabilities and low latency redefine the way urban systems operate. The integration of IoT and 5G brings forth a lot of opportunities but also introduces complex security challenges that demand careful consideration and innovative solutions.

5G technology with IoT is reshaping the landscape of consumer electronics, ushering in a new era of connectivity and innovation. Edge computing plays a pivotal role in the seamless integration of 5G and IoT, ushering a paradigm in how data is processed and utilized within this dynamic ecosystem.

Thus, the integration of 5G and IoT represents a powerful symbiosis that is reshaping the landscape of connectivity and technological innovation.

Security Challenges in 5G Networks

5G technology enables a highly connected environment, integrating smart devices, vehicles, healthcare equipment, *etc.* The speed and capacity of the 5G networks increase the risk of cyberattacks, including DDoS (Distributed Denial of Service) attacks, data breaches, and ransomware. Cybercriminals can exploit the enhanced capabilities of 5G to launch sophisticated and rapid attacks affecting numerous users simultaneously.

Supply chain vulnerabilities are a significant concern due to the involvement of global vendors in building 5G infrastructure. A single compromised component in the supply chain can lead to widespread security weaknesses. Privacy issues arise from the vast amount of data generated by connected devices, raising concerns about unauthorized access to sensitive information. The proliferation of IoT devices on 5G presents security challenges, as many devices lack security features.

Many IoT devices are vulnerable to hacking, like having unsecured doors in the house. The decentralized nature of 5G networks complicates security, with numerous software-based systems requiring monitoring and protection. Location tracking is another concern, as 5G networks pose privacy risks by enabling precise user location identification.

Data collection practices in 5G networks can lead to the creation of detailed user profiles, raising concerns about data usage and protection. Legacy infrastructure and untrusted equipment can introduce vulnerabilities into 5G, carrying over old security issues.

Addressing all these security concerns is essential to ensure the safety and security of our increasingly connected world.

CONCLUDING REMARKS

This chapter provides an overview of 5G Technology in terms of its characteristics, working, and massive MIMO technology. The fusion of 5G and the IoT is reshaping the urban landscape, and security challenges in 5G are also discussed.

EXERCISES

1. Mention the characteristics of 5G technology.
2. How does 5G technology work?
3. What do you mean by MIMO technology? Describe the advantages of MIMO technology in 5G.
4. What do you mean by MM wave band? How does it work in 5G?
5. How does OFDM make 5G functional?
6. What are the security challenges in 5G networks?
7. What is the need for integration of 5G and IoT?

REFERENCES

[1]   G. Camarillo, and Miguel A. García-Martín, "5G mobile and wireless communication technology", *Nokia Research Center,* 2016.

[2]   Available from: https://proceedings.informingscience.org/InSITE2010/InSITE10p267-276Olawale
779.pdf

[3]   J.A. Dias, J.J. Rodrigues, and N. Kumar, "A hybrid system to stimulate selfish nodes to cooperate in
vehicular delay-tolerant networks", *IEEE International Conference on Communications (ICC)*, pp.
5910-5915, 2015.
[http://dx.doi.org/10.1109/ICC.2015.7249264]

CHAPTER 8

Internet of Things

Abstract: The Internet of Things (IoT) is a network comprising things or objects that are assigned unique identities and connected to the Internet. As per the statistics, by 2030, there will be approximately 30 billion devices or things connected to the internet [1]. These networks not only connect things to the Internet but also allow them to communicate and exchange information with each other. To establish connectivity between the various devices and the Internet, IoT uses important protocols such as MQTT, 6LowPAN, Bluetooth, RFID, ZigBee, CoAP, *etc*. IoT is useful in all types of applications, such as healthcare monitoring, agricultural domains, mining, and space applications. IoT real-life application generates a large volume of data, which is analogous to Big Data, which needs to be processed, stored, and analyzed to extract useful information. IoT is shaping the way we live our lives.

Keywords: Bluetooth, CoAP, Gateway, IoT connectivity, IoT WAN, IoT LAN, MQTT, 6LowPAN, RFID, ZigBee.

INTRODUCTION

IoT, as the name suggests, starts with the word 'Internet', which is nothing but a connection of computers as well as computer-oriented devices. The Internet is a global network. Nowadays, the Internet of Things is one of the hottest technologies across the globe. All types of organizations, government or private, and industries are involved in different aspects, such as implementation, business, and research on IoT. Currently, a lot of investments are being made in almost all these organizations for the development of the Internet of Things.

Nowadays, the Internet of Things is becoming more popular in all types of applications, such as healthcare monitoring, agricultural domains, mining, and space applications. Across the world, there has been a lot of interest in developing smart city applications such as smart surveillance to detect if any illegal activity is going on. Next is the smart health application, wherein the patient is allowed to check which hospital provides which type of facility and accordingly makes use of it without physically moving to the required location to get the required information. Similarly, smart parking is another application of IoT, wherein people easily identify free slots and park their vehicles over there, especially during peak hours; otherwise, it is very difficult to identify free parking locations. Next is smart home applications, which may be related to household resource monitoring or taking care of elderly people who are staying alone. Using IoT, it is possible to control or monitor the working of essential household appliances from remote places, and it is even possible to watch remotely whether elderly people are facing any problems at home or not.

IoT is one of the very popular evergreen technologies that make our lives very simple and also enhance the quality of life without much investment. Using IoT, we can connect all of our appliances to the Internet and monitor them remotely. Because of IoT, we can build several multidisciplinary applications in our day-to-day lives.

Equation of IoT

IoT= Physical object +

Controller, Sensor, Actuator +

Internet

IoT is nothing but a connection of computers and computer-oriented devices. The Internet is a global network. Now comes the point: 'Why is IoT needed?'. Very soon, most of the things that we see around us will get interconnected.

Devices used in IoT are categorized into two groups: Basic Devices and Advanced Devices.

  i. Basic Devices: These are devices that only provide the fundamental services to an application, such as sensing useful data or actuating tasks with limited human intervention. These devices are connected to local networks *via* technologies such as ZigBee, Bluetooth, Wi-Fi, cellular networks, *etc*.
 ii. Advanced Devices: The large volume of data that is collected through sensors from various distances for an application requires to be processed to get useful information out of it. Data may also have to be ported to the cloud through a WAN connection. The types of devices that fall under this category are Gateway devices and Cloud Platform.

Deployment can differ for basic and advanced deployment scenarios. Deployment scenarios for basic devices include smart gardening, smart home monitoring, *etc*. In such applications, sensors such as temperature sensors, soil moisture sensors, and humidity sensors are involved, and the central unit takes care of application logic. The central unit can also be connected to WAN.

Deployment scenarios for advanced devices include smart meters. In such applications, meters are installed in houses or organizations for measuring electricity, gas, water, *etc*. Here, the central gateway collects data from the meters from various household and organization premises and then aggregates the data. Finally, the data is sent to either server through a cellular connection for generating the invoices.

Implementation Aspects of IoT

To implement IoT, we need to understand the fundamental basics behind IoT, the basic technology, network connectivity, and the devices required to establish the connection. The Internet is a global network in which different computers are interconnected. IoT is beyond this technology, wherein various things or physical objects that we see around us get interconnected. The things may be fans, lighting systems in a room, refrigerators, and anything in a room, including a microwave oven, television, and so on. Internetworking of devices is not only limited to homes and industries but also extends to various business activities. Now, the question is why this IoT has become so popular? The reason is that IoT provides an advanced level of services to society, businesses, and so on. Numerous IoT-related devices that we use in our daily lives rely on embedded systems, embedded electronics, embedded communication systems, *etc*., so that they make use of some common platforms. Each thing under this network is treated as a node. The outcome of connecting this device is a very large network, which is larger than the normal Internet.

IoT is now used widely in smart homes and smart city applications not only in India but also in the entire globe. In IoT, nodes are interconnected using wireless technologies. As of now, over 9 billion devices are interconnected in IoT networks. Soon, this count may go beyond 20 billion. So, in the near future, billions or trillions of things are going to be interconnected.

There are two different approaches in which IoT can be built. The first one is connecting things to the existing network, and the second approach is to build the network from scratch. Each approach used in building the IoT has its challenges that have to be taken care. In IoT, there can be a variety of devices with different configurations. The unification of all these devices is very much required as IoT is not a single technology. Each of the things in the IoT may be of different configurations, different specifications, and so on. Each of them may be supported by many other technologies, such as cloud computing, big data, machine learning, computer vision, *etc*. So, developing IoT solutions requires expertise from various disciplines, such as computer science, electrical engineering, and mechanical engineering.

The IoT originated in 2000, which is an era of ubiquity wherein connectivity happened from anywhere at any point in time. The result of this is the connection of millions and trillions of things that get connected, including humans. So, very soon, the humans that are connected to things will be outnumbered. Consequently, all these devices will send a lot of data; they have to be handled and analyzed to get useful information. Thus, IoT is going to be one of the complex networks with a much wider scope in comparison to the traditional network. With IoT, various challenges need to be faced, and accordingly, there exists a large number of tools to address these challenges.

To build IoT, we need to use some common enabling technologies, such as RFID (Radio Frequency Identification), nanotechnology, sensors, and smart networks. While building an IoT, there may be several challenges that need to be handled due to its specific characteristics, such as many devices getting interconnected, devices being of limited power, unambiguous naming and addressing of all the devices, mobility of devices, intermittent connectivity between the nodes in the network, *etc*.

The applications of IoT broadly are in areas like business, healthcare, biometrics, facial recognition, inventory tracking, and so on. Nowadays, IoT is used mostly in smart cities, smart health, smart agriculture, supply chain control, forest fire detection, air pollution detection, *etc*.

The evolution of interconnection of various devices started with ATMs (Automatic Teller Machines), followed by the Web, which was used to communicate with people through messages, smart motors for efficient use of electricity, digital locks, smart cities, smart vehicles, smart health, and so on. Applications of IoT are involved in almost all real-world problems, not only in the above common applications but also in handling disaster systems such as earthquake monitoring, water leakage notification, forest fire monitoring, supply chain control, landslide monitoring, intelligent shopping applications, *etc*. IoT market share is shown in Fig. (**1**).

What is required to build IoT? The answer is trillions of sensors, billions of smart systems, and millions of applications. All these devices are interconnected synchronously to build IoT. While framing connectivity between various devices, different technologies to be used are RFID, ZigBee, 6LowPan, LORA, *etc*.

Other technologies used while building IoT are Big Data, sensor networks, and regular wireless networks.

What is the difference between IoT and M2M? In M2M(machine-to-machine) connectivity, communication happens between two machines. IoT has a broader scope than M2M connectivity., In IoT, apart from machine-to-machine interaction, there exists an interaction between things and applications.

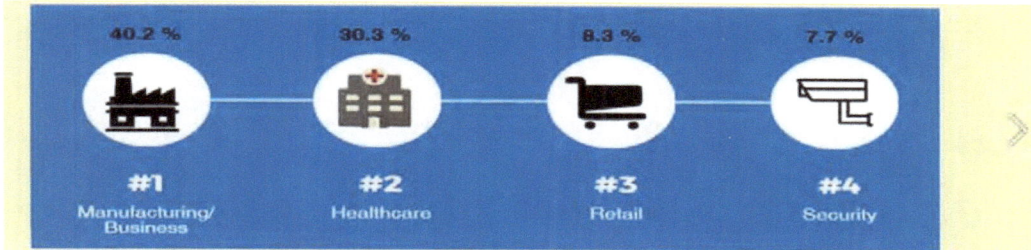

Fig. (1). IoT market share.

As has already been mentioned, due to the variety of technologies used in interconnecting things in IoT, the integration of various connectivity features such as cellular networks, Wi-Fi, Bluetooth Low Energy(BLE), IEEE 802.15.1, IEEE 802.15.4, IEEE 802.15.6, and IEEE 802.16 is very challenging. The main problem is how you are going to deal with the handshake in between. As we have normal Internet computer networks such as LAN, WAN, Gateway, and so on, analogous to IoT, we can have various terminologies, as shown in Fig. (**2**) [1, 2].

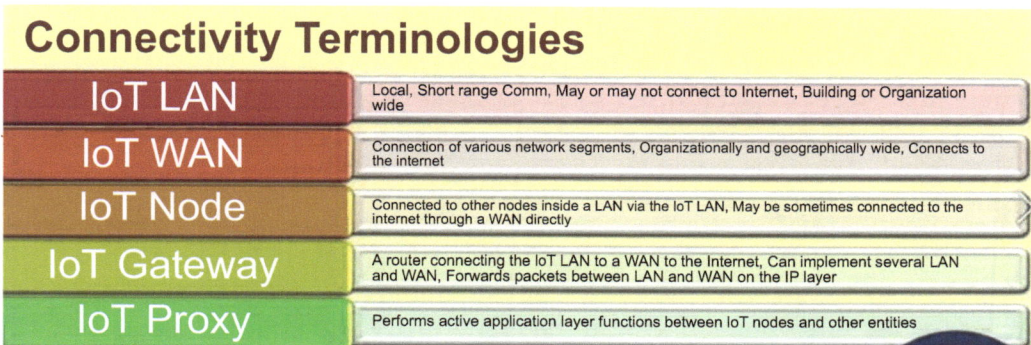

Fig. (2). IoT Connectivity Terminology.

In IoT LAN, each IoT node may have a unique address or local address. Two or more IoT LANs may be interconnected by using IoT gateway. This smart network is called IoT WAN, as shown in Fig. (**3**).

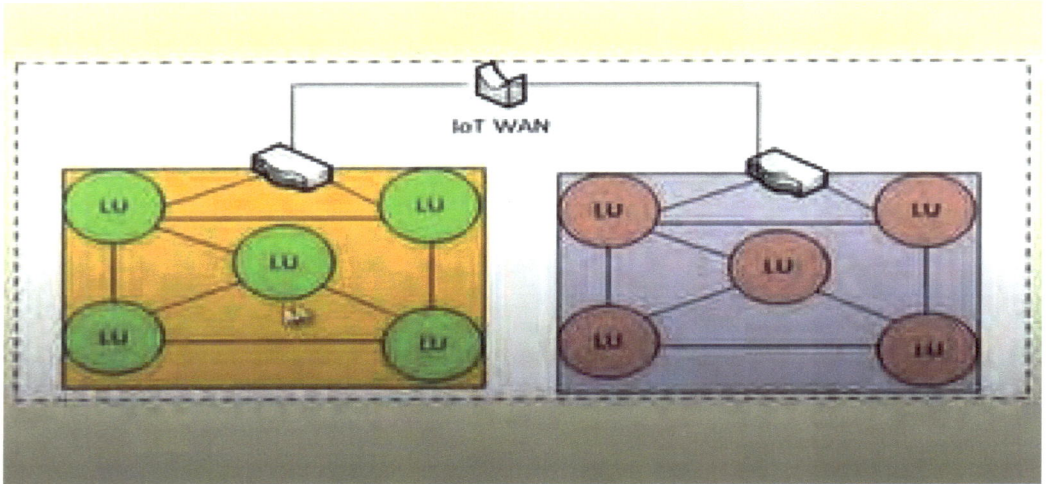

Fig. (3). IoT WAN.

In IoT WAN, under each IoT LAN, the address is unique. But the same address may be reused in another LAN in the same IoT WAN. In that case, the address of repeated IoT addresses will be prefixed with the gateway that is connected to that IoT LAN. Also, there is a proxy, which is used to connect to the external Internet and the proxy is beyond the Gateway. Gateway helps in avoiding the creation of unnecessary addresses and all nodes connect to the Internet *via* the gateway. All the nodes connected in the IoT WAN are connected to the Internet through IoT gateway and IoT routers. Fig. (**4**) shows IoT nodes connected to the Internet through IoT gateway and IoT router. These routers assign the prefix to the gateways that are under them. For example, prefix 1 is assigned to Gateway 1 by Router 1, and prefix 2 is assigned to Gateway 2 by Router 2.

Another important concept here is mobility. When the node changes its location from IoT LAN1 to IoT LAN2, the prefix of the IoT node changes from 1 to 2. This makes IoT LAN safe due to changes in mobility. IoT Gateway WAN takes care of the address changes without changing the LAN address. So, within the LAN, the address remains the same, whereas when the node moves, the address changes. This is how the address changes due to mobility are taken care.

Protocols in IoT

There exists a large number of protocols that are required for connectivity in IoT such as MQTT, 6LowPAN, Bluetooth, RFID, ZigBee, CoAP, *etc*. These protocols are primarily involved in service offerings. All these protocols can be used in both consumer IoTs and industrial IoTs. Consumer IoT means smart home applications, connecting consumer devices, *etc*. Industrial IoT means connecting various industrial machines and medical devices.

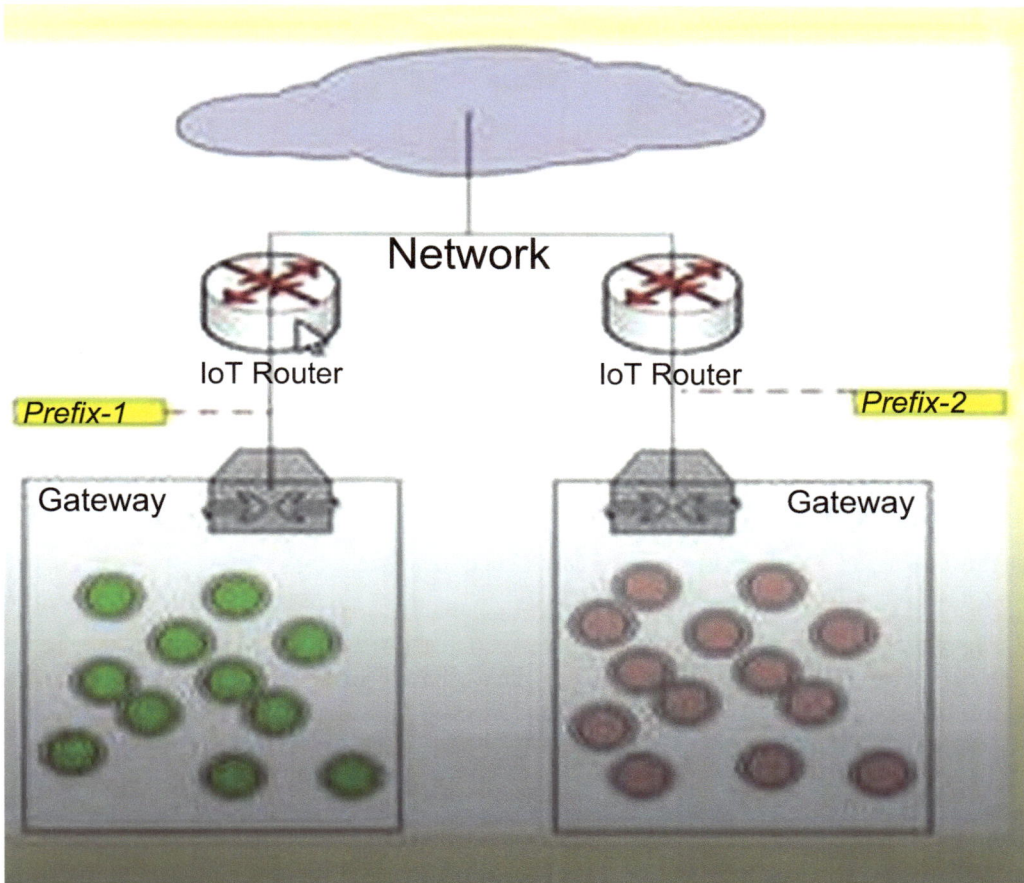

Fig. (4). IoT nodes connected to the Internet through IoT Gateway and IoT Router.

A. ***IEEE 802.15.4:*** This is a well-known standard for Wireless Personal Area Networks (WPANs). IEEE 802.15.4 is mainly designed for low-data rate monitoring and control. For example, it is developed for monitoring personal healthcare applications. It is also used for extended life, low-power consumption applications. It has three main layers, the Physical layer, MAC layer, and Logical Link Control (LLC) and Service Specific Convergence Sublayer (SSCS) layers, that communicate with all upper layers. IEEE 802.15.4 protocol operates in the ISM band standard.

This particular protocol gives specifications for operating with physical, MAC, SSCS, and LLC layers. Here, the focus is on the physical and data link layers of the traditional OSI reference model, as shown in Fig. (**5**).

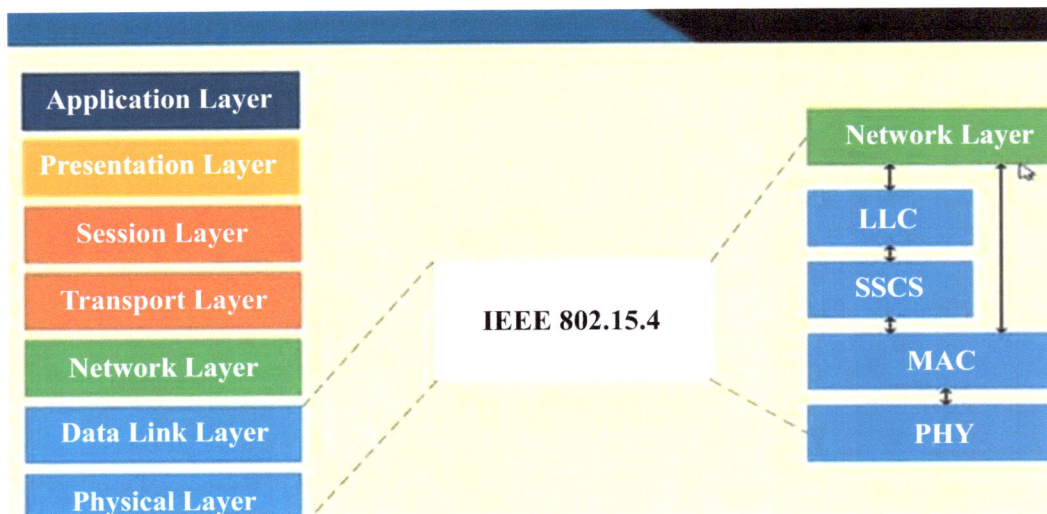

Fig. (5). Mapping Physical and Data link layers of OSI to IEEE 802.15.4.

B. ***ZigBee:*** ZigBee protocol is mainly used for connecting various nodes in the IoT network. It works on top of IEEE 802.15.4. IEEE 802.15.4 is used for establishing connectivity and functionality in the MAC and physical layer. ZigBee protocol uses these functionalities provided by IEEE 802.15.4 to the higher layers (Network layer and above). ZigBee is based on IEEE 802.15.4, but it has its own identity. So, the *ZigBee* protocol operates in layer three and above.

ZigBee protocol uses the top 3 to 4 layers to define additional communication enhancements, such as establishing security and privacy while transmitting data to and from the communication channel. Wireless sensor network applications are an example of utilizing ZigBee for framing mesh topology for communication. Fig. (**6**) shows the position of ZigBee concerning IEEE 802.15.4, whereas IEEE focuses mainly on the physical and MAC layer, while ZigBee is beyond the network layer and the layers above the network layer. This extension is made possible with IEEE 802.15.4 with the help of ZigBee.

ZigBee primarily has 2 components: ZigBee Device Object (ZDO) and Application Support Sublayer (ASS). ZDO is responsible for device management and security policy. The responsibility of ASS is to provide interfacing and control services and to provide a bridge between the network and other services.

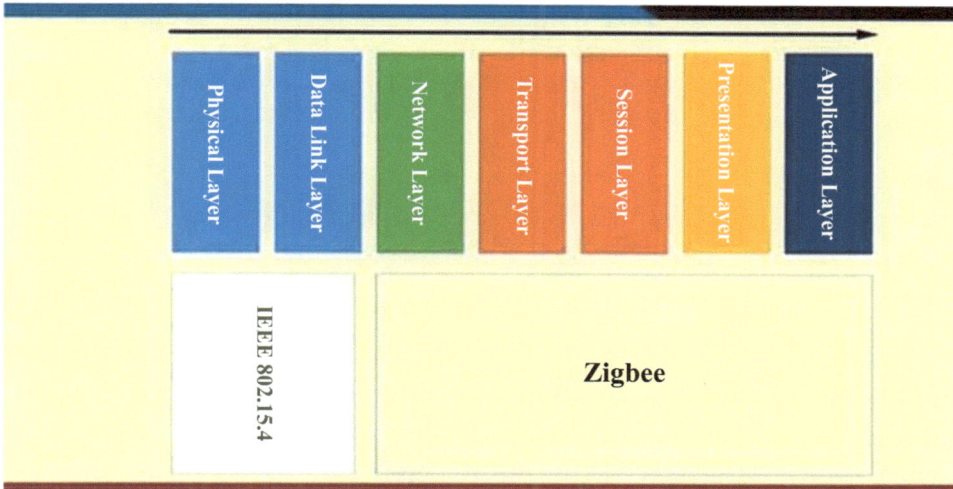

Fig. (6). Position of ZigBee concerning IEEE 802.15.4.

The various topologies ZigBee protocol supports are Star topology, Mesh topology, and Cluster Tree topology, as shown in Fig. (**7**).

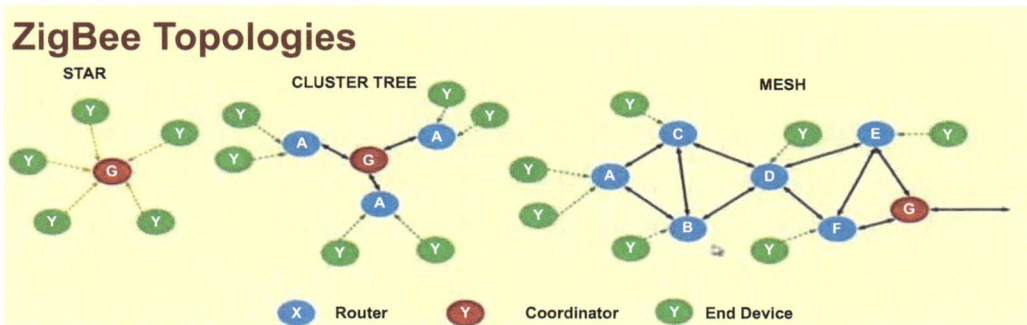

Fig. (7). ZigBee Topologies.

In Star topology, there exist several end devices and a coordinator node. Star topology is best suited for the local area network. In a cluster tree topology, there exist several clusters with cluster heads or routers. Routers form a tree-like structure with the coordinator node, hence the name cluster tree. In mesh topology, routers form a mesh-like structure. In mesh topology, there is a possibility that any node can communicate with any other node in the same network. This is the advantage of mesh topology to improve reliability and fault tolerance. In mesh topology, if the nodes are not in the range or nodes are not reachable, then the messages are relayed through the nearby nodes in the same path, thus allowing the network deployment over long distances. ZigBee mesh networks are self-configuring and self-healing. Self-healing means if any link or node failure occurs in the network, still packets get transmitted through an alternative path. Also, they can configure on their own or they can form the network on their own.

ZigBee Network contains 3 types of nodes: *Coordinator, Router, and End devices.*

a. **ZigBee Coordinator**: This node is the root node of the ZigBee network and acts as a bridge between other similar networks. There exists a single ZigBee coordinator in each ZigBee network, which initiates the network and gathers information about the network under it and information outside it. Also, it takes care of security.
b. **ZigBee Router(ZR):** ZR is capable of relaying information between nodes connected to it and running the applications.
c. **ZigBee End Device(ZED): ZED** is not able to relay information to other devices, but it contains the required functionality to communicate with its parent nodes. This allows the node to be asleep for some time, thus improving the battery lifetime. Compared to ZR and ZC, the storage requirements and the cost of ZED are very low.

ZigBee protocol has several applications, such as it can be used in healthcare monitoring for smart health, building automation, smart home monitoring, smart energy for home energy monitoring, *etc.*

C. *6LoWPAN:* 6LoWPAN is a low-power wireless personal area network where every node has its own IPv6 address. 6LoWPAN protocol runs over IPV6 protocol. It offers radio connectivity over IPV6. IPV6 is a very popular addressing protocol that can be used for addressing IoT devices as IoT connects a very large number of devices.

This protocol allows devices with limited processing ability to transmit information in a wireless medium using Internet protocol IPV6. This protocol allows for connecting low-power devices to the Internet using IPV6 addressing. 6LoWPAN protocol is created out of IETF RFC 6606 and RFC 6606 [3].

Some of the important features of the 6LoWPAN protocol are:

• Allows radios of IEEE 802.15.4 to carry 128-bit addresses of IPV6.
• Allows IEEE 802.15.4 radios to access the Internet using header compression and address translation techniques. This is required because IEEE 802.15.4 is a low-power lightweight protocol, whereas IPV6 is not lightweight.

- Accommodates IPV6 packets in IEEE 802.15.4 packet format. They are compressed and reformatted.

6LoWPAN uses 2 types of addresses: 16-bit short addresses for communicating within the PAN or personal area network and 64-bit extended addresses used for global unique connectivity throughout the network.

Fig. (**8**) shows the 6LoWPAN packet format. As shown in the figure, IEEE 802.15.4 and IPV6 are plumbed together. Concerning IPV6, there are important fields such as source address, destination address, payload length, and other fields, and for IEEE 802.15.4, the source and destination fields together use 128 bits and PAN ID, which is a unique ID corresponding to personal area network and other fields.

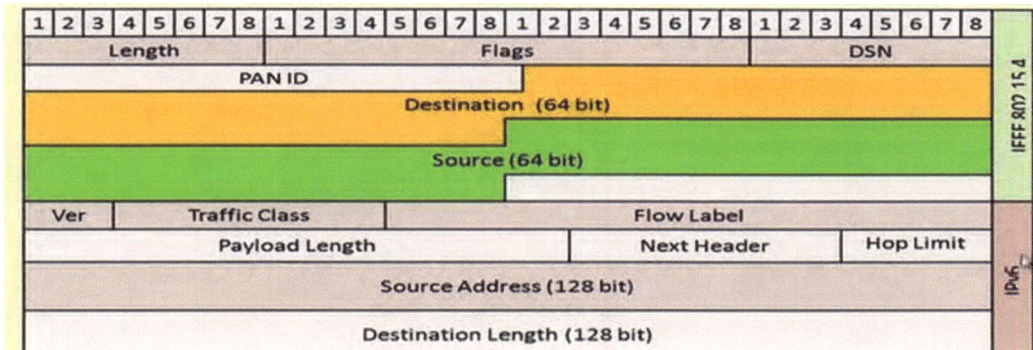

Fig. (8). 6LoWPAN Packet format.

As 6LoWPAN contains a strong network layer component, it takes care of routing. The most popular routing here is mesh-based routing. This routing happens in the context of PAN topology and is based on IPV6. LOADng and RPL are the two routing protocols used in 6LoWPAN and 6LoWPAN, as shown in Fig. (**9**).

Routing in 6LoWPAN contains PAN and IPV6. With the help of a coordinator or gateway, as shown in Fig. (**9**), PAN is connected to the IPv6 network domain.

a. **LOADng Protocol:** This protocol is derived from the AODV protocol, which is used for routing in MANETs. The extended version of the AODV protocol is LOADng, which is suitable for routing in IoT. The responsibility of LOADng protocol is to generate a Route Request(RREQ) for discovering the route to the destination. Once the RREQ is received by the destination node, a Route Reply (RREP) gets forwarded to the source on a unicast hop-by-hop basis. Route Error (RERR) message is returned to the originator to inform the route breakage in case the route detected is broken. To minimize the problem of flooding and RREQ overhead, optimized flooding is supported. Here, intermediate routers are prohibited from responding to RREQs. Only the destination node is responsible for responding to RREQs.

b. **RPL Protocol:** This protocol originated from Distance Vector IPv6 routing protocol for low power and lossy networks. RPL follows low-rate beaconing. The beaconing rate increases only when the link or node in a route is down. With RPL protocol, routing information is included in the datagram itself, and it makes use of proactive as well as reactive routing. RPL supports message confidentiality and integrity. Routing optimization objectives of RPL include minimizing energy and latency.

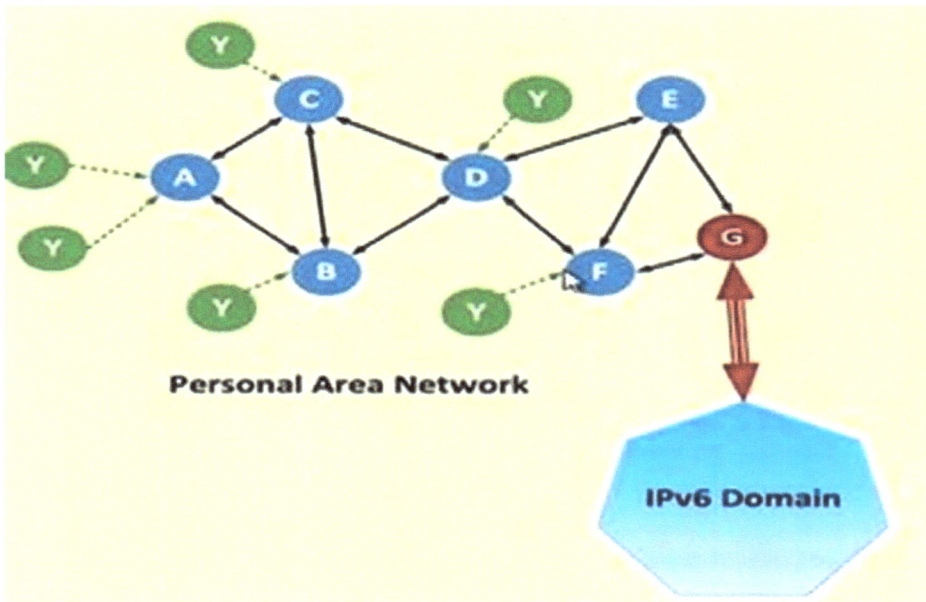

Fig. (9). Routing in 6LoWPAN.

D. *RFID:* RFID stands for Radio Frequency Identification (RFID). This is one of the very popular protocols used, especially in shopping malls, workplaces, *etc.*, wherein an RFID reader is used to scan the RFID tags. RFID is like Sensor Networks, ZigBee, and IEEE 802.15.4, which are used for establishing connectivity in IoT applications. RFID tags contain the data, and RFID readers detect the tag and process the information from the tags when in range, as shown in Fig. (**10**). Data is digitally encoded in these RFID tags. This data can be read from the RFID tags by the RFID reader. This is like the barcoding schemes used in libraries and the QR coding schemes used in shopping malls. However, RFID tags function slightly differently from these technologies.

An integrated circuit and an antenna are the two components of every RFID tag. Basically, it is a small tag containing small integrated circuitry with an antenna embedded inside the tag. The antenna is used for communication outside the tag, and the circuitry stores the information in that tag. RFID can be like a smart card for storing, for example, employees' identification information.

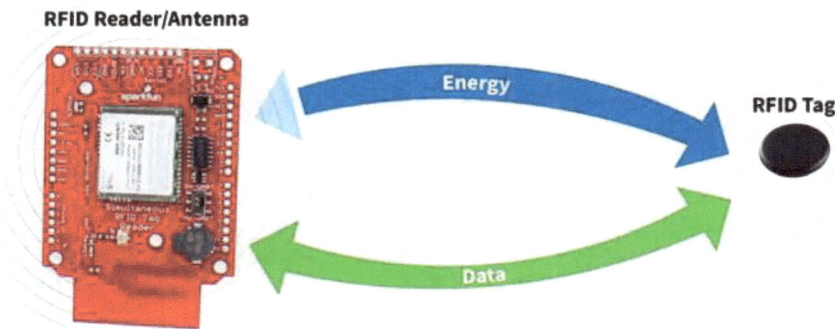

Fig. (10). RFID Tag and Reader.

To protect against various environmental conditions, RFID tags are covered by a protective material, which also acts as a shield. These tags may be active or passive. Most widely, RFID tags are passive. Active tags have their power supply, while passive tags must be powered by a reader inductively before they can transmit information. The working principle of RFID is like its predecessor, Automatic Identification and Data Capturing (AIDC). AIDC does object data capturing and mapping of the collected data to the computer systems with little or no human interventions. RFID uses radio waves to perform AIDC operations, whereas AIDC uses wired communication. So, the concept of RFID is adapted from its predecessor, AIDC.

Fig. (**11**) shows the working of RFID. It consists of tags attached to clothing in a shopping mall, for example. RFID tag consists of a circuitry, a coining mechanism, and a cover. This cover may be some kind of polymer or plastic, and the circuitry is stored in that tag. In Fig. (**11**), the first half shows the RFID reader, and the next half shows the RFID tag.

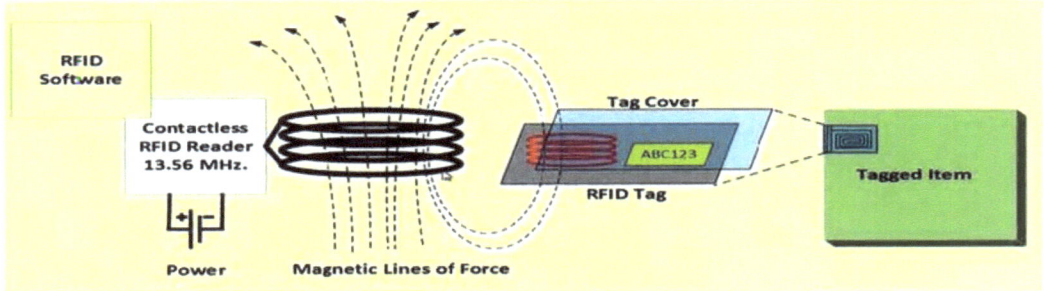

Fig. (11). RFID Tag and Reader.

RFID reader has software, a source of power supply, and a coil. The coil in the reader has a magnetic coil. The magnetic inductive effect is created inside the RFID reader, due to which the data stored in the small chip inside the RFID tag gets transferred to the RFID reader [4].

RFIDs are useful in supporting IoT applications such as asset tracking, inventory management, personal tracking, supply chain management, controlling access to restricted areas, *etc.*

E. ***Bluetooth Technology:*** Bluetooth technology is designed mainly for short-range personal area communications. For example, if we need to replace wired PAN connectivity between various devices, then Bluetooth can be used, which replaces the wired connection with a wireless connection. Applications of Bluetooth include connecting various peripheral devices to personal computers to transfer data between two mobile devices.

Bluetooth has an entirely different protocol stack as compared to other protocols. One of the important features of Bluetooth is it ensures a high level of security, and another distinctive feature is that Bluetooth helps in forming Ad Hoc networks. Bluetooth operates in the frequency range of 2.4 to 2.484 GHz, and it supports 3Mbps data rate and above.

Bluetooth operates in different classes of radios: class 1, class 2, and class 3. Class 3 radios have a range of up to 1 meter or 3 feet, Class 2 radios have a range of up to 10 meters or 30 feet, and Class 1 radios have a range of up to 100 meters or 300 feet. Fig. (**12**) shows the Bluetooth protocol stack. It consists of the physical layer, baseband layer, L2CAP layer, other protocol layers, and then, finally, the application layer. The protocol layer consists of various protocols such as RFCOMM, LLC, Telephony Service Discovery, *etc.* All these protocols are mapped to traditional OSI layers: physical layer, datalink layer, middleware layer, and application layer.

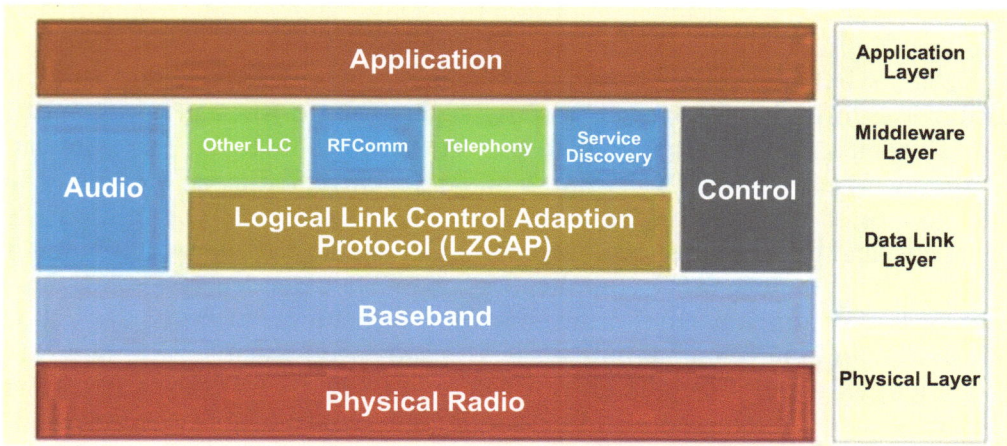

Fig. (12). Bluetooth protocol stack.

Just above the physical layer, there is the baseband layer, which manages the physical channels and the links. Other services of the baseband layer include error correction, hop selection, Bluetooth security, *etc*.

L2CAP stands for Logical Link Control and Adaptation Protocol. It provides both connection-oriented and connection-less services to upper-layer protocols. Multiplexing, multiple logical connections between devices, is made possible with the help of the L2CAP protocol. It is also responsible for segmentation and reassembly operations.

RFComm (Radio Frequency and Communication) protocol is responsible for replacing existing serial cables with a Bluetooth wireless connection. RFComm is the emulation of the traditional serial port RS-232. RFComm protocol is designed to provide emulated RS-232 serial ports over Bluetooth connections. RFComm is similar to TCP protocol (simple, reliable communication protocol), which supports up to 60 connections between two Bluetooth devices.

Advancements in IoT

With the current technological advancements, we are now in the golden age of IoT technology, which means transformation in almost all industries is happening to improve productivity by storing and processing data in a distributed manner.

IoT is a technology that includes a wide collection of interconnected devices that can communicate with each other. These connected devices are smart enough to gather and analyze information and make decisions accordingly.

The usage of IoT is increasingly multifold nowadays, and the future appears to be completely dependent on such devices. IoT makes our lives simpler by decreasing human interventions and increasing efficiency by developing and applying multilevel algorithms. With such a massive increase in the networks and the devices connected to such networks, concerns about security in such environments become inevitable. Based on the recent statistics on the sale of IoT devices reported from Gartner, it is expected to be more than one million USD every hour, and the predicted spending for 2023 was $1.1 trillion, continuing the trend of increased growth. The application of IoT is extended into the fields of agriculture, environment monitoring, units where manufacturing is taken to the next level with smart connectivity of devices, massive smart cities, and, most important of all, the healthcare industry. These IoT devices form a smart grid type of infrastructure, which consists of simple things such as a smart toaster used at home or very complexthings such as a heart monitoring device implanted within the heart or automobiles connected to smart computers, all of which provide a better and efficient digital experience. As per the International Telecommunication Union (ITU), the vision towards IoT, as mentioned, stands as follows: "technology to provide connectivity to anything". The data flow between these devices in IoT would be huge and essential, as all of them communicate with each other to make many of the critical decisions. According to Fortune Business Insights, the global IoT market size stood at USD 250.72 billion in 2019 and is projected to reach USD 1,463.19 billion by 2027 [5], exhibiting a Compound Annual Growth Rate (CAGR) of 24.9% during the forecast period, as shown in Fig. (**13**).

There is a tremendous growth in IMT traffic, which in turn influences the technical requirements such as adaptation of devices with enhanced capabilities, increased video usage, device proliferation, evolution of new applications, *etc*. One of the standard ITU-R M.2370 tells us that global IMT traffic will grow 10-100 from 2020 to 2030. Fig. (**14**) shows the prediction of global mobile subscriptions from 2020 to 2030.

In the above figure, the x-axis shows the years from 2020 to 2030. The Y-axis shows the number of various kinds of mobile devices predicted to be subscribed. In each year, under a particular column, 3 types of devices, such as smartphones, tablets, and feature phones, are represented in terms of a billion devices. For example, in the year 2020, a total of 10.8 billion such devices were subscribed. Also, it is predicted that by 2026, feature phones will vanish. This means that feature phone traffic will be dominated by smartphones, tablets, and other smart devices. It is expected that in 2026, traffic that is generated by feature phones will vanish, and it will be dominated by the traffic generation by smart homes and tablets.

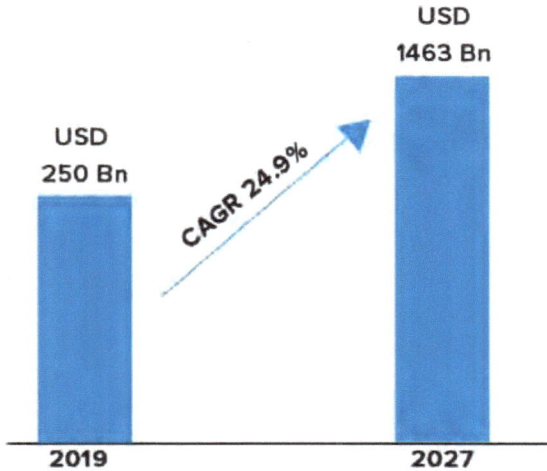

Fig. (13). Global IoT market Statistics [6].

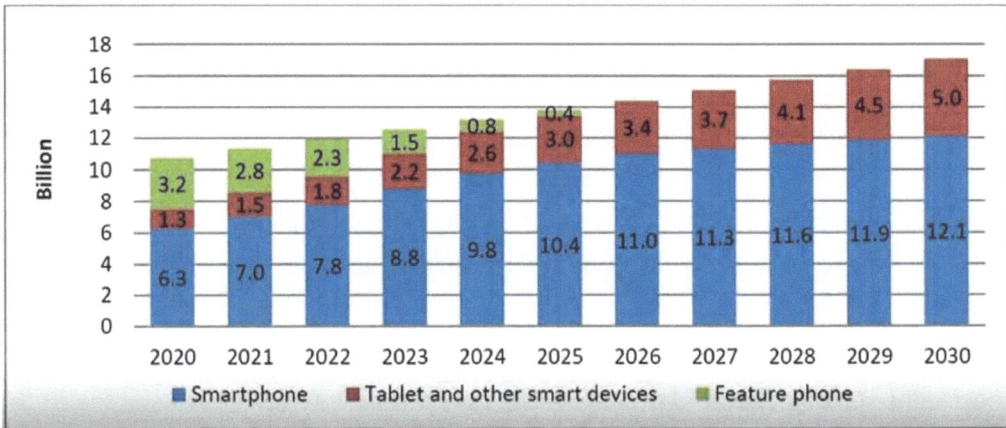

Fig. (14). Prediction of global mobile subscription from 2020 to 2030.

About Use Cases and Example Use Case

IoT enables the power of the Internet and analytics to be given to the physical objects or assets of the real world. In IoT, the physical world needs to be connected to the Internet to send the data that needs to be processed in real time. This data can be used to control the object itself or smartly control some other objects. Thus, IoT is a network of connected objects that can exchange information *via* the Internet. Based on IoT connectivity technology and the availability of devices that support connectivity, it is possible to make use cases for many real-world problems. Examples of use cases are in home automation, buildings, security, healthcare, infrastructure, *etc.*

How the IoT works is quite simple. The three important steps are specified below:

1. Initially, IoT acquires basic data such as names, addresses, *etc.*, and attributes of real-time objects in terms of automatic identification by means of RFID tags and sensor networks. For all these objects, smartphones can be used as a central hub.
2. The information retrieved by step 1 can be further integrated with the help of the latest communication technologies to integrate the information for restoring fundamental resource services.
3. Finally, the integrated information needs to be processed and analyzed to realize the intelligent decision and then control the physical world by making use of cloud infrastructure, fuzzy recognition, big data analytics, semantic analysis, and so forth.

The above steps can be mapped to 3 layers: Physical, Network, and Application. In the lowest layer or physical layer, data is collected from the world using sensors (uniquely identifiable "things") and transmitted to internet devices (like smartphones). After that, through transmission lines (like fiber-optic cable), it goes to the network layer, where all the data is managed separately (stream analytics and data analytics) from the raw data. Next, all the managed information is sent to the application layer for proper utilization of the data collected based on the application [5, 7].

In the IoT application setup, a network of various devices interacting with each other and their environmentare framed. As the interaction happens in terms of various hardware platforms, it may lead to interoperability and connectivity issues. These issues need to be taken care of by building common infrastructure or autonomous interactive objects. The most commonly used platforms are Arduino and Raspberry Pi.

In IoT, building a use case for an application is a research strategy that investigates a phenomenon within its real-life context. Use cases are based on an in-depth identification of a single individual, group, or event to explore the causes of underlying principles. For example, one of the most promising IoT use cases is creating smart cities, smart healthcare, or precision agriculture.

IoT prototyping is the action of experimenting and implementing design ideas into preliminary versions of a finished product. Essentially, it involves trying out and testing different ways to bring something from the planning phase to reality.

Having an idea leads to the IoT prototyping process, which is the most crucial step before any IoT product is mass-produced and sold to people. The purpose of prototype building is to test your concept with an actual target audience, to find out about all necessary parameters for your IoT device deployment, to become aware of all technical requirements, and to find out if they can meet your expectations [8, 9].

You may want to create an IoT device just for yourself or may want to produce millions of products; in both cases, the most sensible thing to do is to start making a prototype. You will inevitably come across problems in your design that you need to change and iterate. Doing this with a single object is trivial compared to modifying hundreds or thousands of products. The prototype is optimized for ease and speed of development and the ability to change and modify it.

The main steps involved in developing a use case for the prototype are shown in Fig. (**15**).

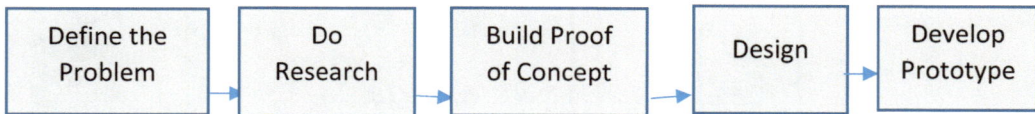

Fig. (15). IoT Prototyping Steps.

Example Prototype: IoT Indoor Localization Using Bluetooth Low Energy (BLE)

  i. **Objective:-** To create a navigation system that helps navigate users through a particular building using an Android app.
 ii. **Scope of Project:** Correct identification of user location while moving between three BLE beacons can be considered a successful demonstration of Proof of Concept, which can be scaled if needed. This project is compatible with only Android smartphones.
iii. **Hardware and Software Requirements: -** ESP32 and battery Laptop with Arduino IDE Android Smartphone.
 iv. Abstract Architecture:

Fig. (**16**) shows the IoT prototype design or abstract architecture.

Data Handling and Analysis for IoT

In the previous sections, IoT is explained in terms of the interconnection of various devices such as sensors, actuators, mobiles, Wi-Fi, and other communication devices. All these devices produce huge amounts of data. IoT is highly data-intensive, which means IoT is used to gather huge amounts of data from various applications. IoT produces a large volume of data that needs to be handled as well as analyzed properly to get sensitive information out of it so that things can be made much more efficient and more and more IoT devices can be deployed. So, two important goals behind data handling and analysis for IoT are: 1. Data has to be handled properly, and 2. The generated data, which is collected either through centralized fashion or through distributed fashion, must be analyzed properly to sense it to make things work better.

Fig. (15). IoT Prototyping Steps.

There are various ways in which the data can be handled. Data handling ensures that the data from the IoT-based setup is archived and stored properly and disposed of safely and securely during and after the completion of any IoT project. To achieve this, standard policies or procedures should be followed electronically or non-electronically. In most of the IoT projects, the data that is generated will contain several features that are analogous to the features of the Big Data. What is Big Data? In simple terms, Big Data is nothing but data that is extraordinarily big in different ways. Due to heavy traffic generated by IoT devices, huge volumes of data will be created by different sensors and other devices continuously in the network. For example, suppose there is a camera sensor that is supposed to collect images continuously; there may be a large number of images generated or sensed by the camera in an hour. In this way, if the process of collecting the data is continuous in a day, a month, or a year, then a large volume of data gets collected. This is called Big Data.

The large volume of the data that is collected needs to be stored and then analyzed to obtain useful information or knowledge. Also, once that data is no more required, we need to look into the process of disposing of the data. So, all these steps are required when an IoT is used for collecting data from real-world applications. The large volume of data that is collected from IoT devices is said to be Big Data. The following is the standard definitions for Big Data as per NIST:

'Big Data shall mean that data of which it's volume, acquisition speed, or data representation limits the capacity of using traditional relational methods to conduct the effective analysis with important horizontal zoom technologies' [As per National Institute of Standard Technology (NIST)] [10].

The data that is generated from IoT are of two types:

i. Structured Data: The data that is easily organized, stored in relational databases, and which queried is known as structured data. There is very limited data; maybe around 20% of data collected from IoT across the world belong to this category. For Example, data relating to student information systems, banking systems, *etc.*
ii. Unstructured Data: IoT systems produce mostly unstructured data, which cannot be stored in the relational database. It is very huge in size. Most of the data collected from IoT, *i.e.*, around 80% of the data available in the world,belongs to this category. For example, data from video, audio, speech, YouTube, telescope, camera, *etc.*

What are the characteristics of Big Data? Big data is characterized by the 7 V's: Volume, Velocity, Variety, Variability, Veracity, Visualization, and Value.

• *Volume:* This means the quantity of data generated is very huge. For example, from YouTube, the data generated may be in terabytes.
• *Velocity:* The speed of generation of data is velocity. Data processing time is reduced day by day to handle real-time services. Previous batch processing techniques are unable to process huge velocity of data. The data generated by IoT devices, which include mobile phones and sensors, produce data at a very high rate.
• *Variety:* The category to which the data belongs is variety. Most of the data that is generated by the IoT is either unstructured or semi-structured. Also, there is no restriction on the data formats. For example, data may be an image, text file, SMS, video, audio, pdf, *etc.* All these data in large volume and high velocity go

through the same communication channel.

- *Variability:* This means the data whose meaning is constantly changing depending on the context. For example, language processing data is completely different from multimedia data.
- *Veracity: It* refers to the biases, noise, and abnormality in the data. Veracity is not just about data quality; it is also about data understandability.
- *Visualization:* This means how to present the data either in pictorial or in graphical format. It enables the decision-makers to see analytics presented visually, changing depending on the context. For example, the visualization of language processing data is completely different from multimedia data.
- *Value:* Value is nothing but extracting important information from the scattered data. It includes a huge volume and variety of data. Further, it is easy to access and deliver quality analytics that enable decisions.

Data Handling Technologies in IoT

What are the data-handling technologies used in IoT?

There are several technologies used for handling data in IoT.

Cloud Computing

One of the most used technologies is cloud computing. The cloud has several essential characteristics: on-demand service, broad network access, resource pooling, rapid elasticity, *etc.* Cloud provides 3 basic service models. They are Infrastructure as a Service (IaaS), Platform as a Service (PaaS), and Software as a Service(SaaS).

Data Centers

These are mainly used for storing, organizing, and managing large volumes of data, providing necessary processing capabilities, replicating the data to take the backup, discovering problems associated with business operations, and providing sufficient network infrastructure, *etc* [11].

Fig. (**17**) shows the flow of the data from the generation analysis.

As shown in Fig. (**17**), first, the data is generated, and acquisition of the data takes place, followed by storage of the data and finally, analysis. Data gets generated by the users of an enterprise or through IoT devices, biomedical devices, or some other means. In the second stage, the acquisition of the data happens through data collection, data transportation, and pre-processing. After the acquisition stage, storage of the data happens by using the Hadoop MapReduce Framework or

NoSQL database systems. Finally, the stored data is analyzed using Bloom's filter, parallel computing, or Hashing and Indexing.

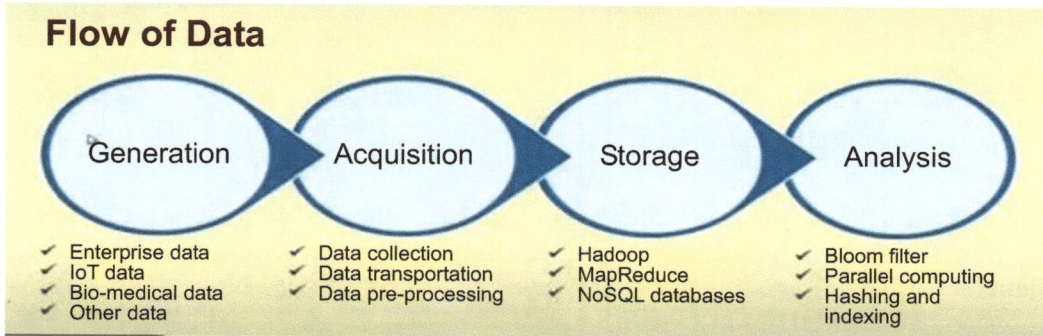

Fig. (17). Flow of the data.

Real-World IoT Applications

IoT plays a vital role in our day-to-day lives as it transforms industry by improving efficiency. The application of IoT is evolving widely in areas such as agriculture, healthcare, and industrial automation. The IoT is a global infrastructure for the information society, enabling advanced services by interconnecting (physical and virtual) things based on existing and evolving interoperable information and communication technologies. Things in IoT have unique identities and can perform sensing, actuating, and monitoring capabilities. Here, sensors get information about the surroundings, such as pushbutton, light-sensitive, and humidity and temperature sensors. On the other hand, actuators respond to decisions made based on sensor values. Examples of actuators are solenoids, stepper motors, and DC motors.

Agricultural Internet of Things and Decision Support for Precision Smart Farming: A Use Case

The integration of wireless sensors with agricultural and cloud platforms aids in the collection of essential environmental data. Sensors will generate massive amounts of data, which must be gathered, saved, shared, processed, analyzed, fused, and interpreted to translate data into new knowledge and action. Fig. (**18**) shows the agricultural IoT model [12].

One of the eminent sectors where IoT has immensely contributed is precision agriculture, at various stages of pre-harvest, during harvest, and post-harvest. There are numerous ways in which smart sensing can enhance various agricultural practices. It can optimize resource management, ensure food safety and a transparent food supply chain, provide farmer and crop insurance, and yield a hassle-free land registry [13, 14]. Customers also prefer to have transparency and knowledge of the food they are consuming in terms of organic crops [15].

Fig. (18). Agricultural IoT model.

The current IoT architecture adopts a centralized authority, which leads to a single point of failure [16, 17]. The emergence of decentralized ledger technology like blockchain can resolve this issue. However, the integration of blockchain and IoT poses several challenges [18 - 20].

CONCLUDING REMARKS

This chapter provides the basics of IoT, IoT connectivity, and IoT use cases along with the working of sample use cases. IoT prototyping is illustrated for real-life examples in terms of architecture and design. Also, some of the important protocols for establishing the connectivity between IoT devices and the Internet are discussed.

EXERCISES

1. What is IoT? Mention the need for IoT.
2. Why the name "Internet of Things"?
3. Differentiate between basic and advanced devices in IoT.
4. What are the key technologies used in forming IoT?
5. Illustrate the growth of IoT in terms of mobile subscription.
6. What do you mean by prototyping in IoT? Why is it needed? Mention the steps involved in making a prototype.
7. By taking an example use case, illustrate the steps involved in making the objects smarter by using an IoT.
8. What is the difference between ZigBee and IEEE 802.15.4 Wireless protocols?
9. What is the need for the 6LoWPAN protocol? How does it work?
10. "IoT technology currently is in its golden age": justify the statement.
11. Design an IoT prototype in terms of abstract architecture, for example, a real-life use case of your choice.
12. Demonstrate the flow of Big Data from the generation stage to the analysis stage.
13. With the help of a use case, demonstrate the IoT in real-world applications.

REFERENCES

[1] "Internet of Things (IoT)", *statistics & facts | Statista.*, 2025.

[2] Available from: https://appinventiv.com/blog/emerging-iot-technologies-in-coming-years/

[3] P. Thubert, Ed. "IPv6 over low-power wireless personal area network (6LoWPAN) selective fragment recovery" Cisco Systems, 2020.

[4] Nan Li, Yi Mu, W. Susilo and V. Varadharajan, "Secure RFID ownership transfer protocols", Springer, 2013.

[5] C. Pfister, "Getting Started with the Internet of Things", *O'Reilly Sixth*, 2018.

[6] Available from: https://www.globenewswire.com/en/news-release/2021/04/08/2206579

[7] A. Bahga, and V. Madisetti, "Internet of things: A hands-on approach", 2014.

[8] Available from: https://www.thisisdmg.com/en/services/digital-products-iot/

[9] M. Sharma, "IoT device management: streamlining connectivity in connected world", DZone, 2023.

[10] Available from: https://www.digimat.in/nptel/courses/video/106105166/L55.html

[11] M. Chen, S. Mao, Y. Zhang, and C.M.Leung. Victor, "Big Data", In: *Springer Science and Business Media LLC*, 2014.

[12] L. Colizzi, D. Caivano, C. Ardito, G. Desolda, A. Castrignanò, and M. Matera, *Introduction to agricultural IoT. In: Agricultural Internet of Things and Decision Support for Precision Smart Farming.* Elsevier, 2020.
[http://dx.doi.org/10.1016/B978-0-12-818373-1.00001-9]

[13] J. Xie, C. Wan, A. Tolón Becerra, and M. Li, "Streamlining traceability data generation in apple production using integral management with machine-to-machine connections", *Agronomy (Basel),* vol. 12, no. 4, p. 921, 2022.
[http://dx.doi.org/10.3390/agronomy12040921]

[14] I. Ehsan, M. Irfan Khalid, L. Ricci, J. Iqbal, A. Alabrah, S. Sajid Ullah, and T.M. Alfakih, "A conceptual model for blockchain-based agriculture food supply chain system", *Sci. Program.*, vol. 2022, pp. 1-15, 2022.
[http://dx.doi.org/10.1155/2022/7358354]

[15] X. Lin, S.C. Chang, T.H. Chou, and S.C. Chen, "Ruangkanjanases a. consumers' intention to adopt blockchain food traceability technology towards organic food products", *Int. J. Environ. Res. Public Health,* 2021.

[16] T.M. Fernández-Caramés, and P. Fraga-Lamas, "A review on the use of blockchain for the internet of things", *IEEE Access,* vol. 6, pp. 32979-33001, 2018.
[http://dx.doi.org/10.1109/ACCESS.2018.2842685]

[17] P. Gupta, V. Dedeoglu, S.S. Kanhere, and R. Jurdak, "TrailChain: Traceability of data ownership across blockchain-enabled multiple marketplaces", *J. Netw. Comput. Appl.*, vol. 203, p. 103389, 2022.
[http://dx.doi.org/10.1016/j.jnca.2022.103389]

[18] MA Uddin, A Stranieri, I Gondal, and V Balasubramanian, "A survey on the adoption of blockchain in IoT: challenges and solutions", *Blockchain: Research and Applications,* 2021.
[http://dx.doi.org/10.1016/j.bcra.2021.100006]

[19] I. Butun, and P. Osterberg, "A review of distributed access control for blockchain systems towards securing the internet of things", *IEEE Access,* vol. 9, pp. 5428-5441, 2021.
[http://dx.doi.org/10.1109/ACCESS.2020.3047902]

[20]   Z. Rahman, X. Yi, S.T. Mehedi, R. Islam, and A. Kelarev, "Blockchain applicability for the internet of things: performance and scalability challenges and solutions", *Electronics (Basel),* vol. 11, no. 9, p. 1-16, 2022.
[http://dx.doi.org/10.3390/electronics11091416]

CHAPTER 9

Fundamentals of 6G Networks

Abstract: 6G is the successor of the 5G cellular network. It is one of the ongoing research areas whose deployment started recently. It makes use of different potential technologies and Terahertz communication. There are a lot of research opportunities in 6G as it is still in the implementation stage. The architecture of 6G is wider. This means the architecture of Terahertz communication covers space, air, ground, and underwater networks, and all segments of the communication network come together and work under the same umbrella, framing ubiquitous connectivity. Potential 6G technology includes 6G with full integration of AI with big data analytics, novel radio access technology, Super Massive MIMO, and quantum computing. The targetted full-fledged deployment of 6G is expected or ITM (International Mobile Telecommunication) by 2030.

Keywords: 6G, 5G, 4G, Super massive MIMO, Terahertz communication.

INTRODUCTION

With this upcoming wireless network, several ambitious key possibilities of 6G exist for the users. They are as follows:

i. The peak data rate that is targeted for 6G is in Terabytes, which is approximately 100 times that of 5G. So there is a tremendous increase in data rate of 6G. The requirement of one user's data rate is approximately 1GB, which is 10 times greater than that of 5G wireless networks.
ii. The range of frequency targeted for 6G is 0.1 to 10 THz (Terahertz). As the frequency targeted in 6G is very high, several challenges need to be addressed due to this.
iii. The spectrum efficiency of 6G is 5 to 10 times as much as that of 5G.
iv. Operates at very high mobility.
v. Latency could be very low: Whenever there is high mobility in the wireless network, the latency could be very low, which is in the order of 10 to 100 microseconds.
vi. The connectivity density of 6G could be at least 10 times the connectivity density of 5G.

vii. Energy efficiency is also required to be at least 10 times higher than that of 5G technology.

viii. Substantially high throughput.

ix. Enhanced data security.

x. Ubiquitous connectivity: Ubiquitous connectivity is needed in 6G to support AI-integrated communication.

Comparison of 6G with 4G and 5G

Table **1** shows the comparison of 6G with 5G and 4G in terms of data rate, AI support, extended reality, satellite communications, and so forth:

Table 1. Comparison of 6G with 4G and 5G wireless networks.

Type of Network	THz Communication	Haptic Communication	AI Integrated	Extended Reality	Satellite Communication
4G	Does not support Terahertz communication; instead, it supports from 2.4GHz to 5 GHz	Does not support Haptic Communication	Integration of Machine Learning and Deep Learning is not there	Does not support extended reality	Does not support Satellite communication
5G	Marginal support for Terahertz communication, *i.e.*, from 28 GHz to 30 GHz	Marginal Support for Haptic Communication	Marginal support for AI is provided	Marginal support for extended reality	Does not support Satellite communication
6G	Supports substantially high frequency for THz communication from 0.1 THz to 10THz.	Substantial support for Haptic Communication	Targeted with complete implementation of AI	Full-fledged support is provided for extended reality	Support Satellite communication

6G ELECTROMAGNETIC SPECTRUM

For 4G LTE, around 6GHz of frequency is supported whereas, for 5G networks, the targeted frequency is around 30GHz. However, for 6G, what we can expect is beyond 100 GHz of frequency to 10 THz. It is very difficult to design the hardware components that utilize high frequency as it may damage the system. So initially, people targeted designing equipment that utilized less frequency of 6G spectrum, *i.e.*, around 100 GHz to 300 GHz. Later, based on the requirements, they started increasing the frequency range, for example, from 300 GHz to 3 THz. As per the literature, it is found that generally, this frequency range is not as harmful as Xray and Gamma-ray frequencies, which have a frequency of 10^{15} to

10^{18}, respectively, which can damage the human body cells. So, the frequency range of up to 3 THz is still under study as to whether Terahertz communication can damage human body cells. One of the advantages of Terahertz communication is that we can achieve throughput. Some of the important features of 6G are discussed below:

i. With the Terahertz frequency range, there will be more bandwidth, so we can achieve very high data rates. *i.e.*, the data rate will be in terms of Terabits per second.
ii. There could be a chance of high path loss rising from high frequency. Due to this problem, it is not possible to transmit signals over longer distances. This could be one of the disadvantages of Terahertz frequency. So, 6G can transmit over shorter distances compared to 4G and 5G. Wider coverage is a challenge. This disadvantage can be overcome by using more towers with beam-forming antennas to encompass the path losses.

6G CHALLENGES

i. **Atmospheric attenuation or atmospheric absorption:** As the frequency increases, the overall attenuation also increases. This means that for lower frequencies, such as 6 GHz to 120 GHz, the atmospheric attenuation is not that high, whereas for frequency above 100 GHz, the attenuation increases rapidly, as shown in Fig. (**1**). This increase in attenuation will deteriorate or degrade our signal. So this means that we not be able to receive the signal with a higher signal-to-noise ratio. This will degrade the Quality of Service.
ii. **Surface scattering:** Most of the lower frequency signals appear smoothly on most of the surfaces. There can be minor scattering but not much trouble with lower frequency, whereas, with the Terahertz spectrum, there is significant diffuse scattering and strong specular reflections. So this can be a major trouble that can degrade our signal quality.
iii. **Partition and penetration losses:** Partition and penetration losses are substantially high as the frequency increases. The higher the frequency, the higher the attenuation in 6G. Also, it depends on the thickness of the material used. The larger the thickness, the larger the attenuation. For example, if we consider a glass or glass wall, we will see an attenuation of 15 to 28 DB (Decibel) based on what frequency we employ and the thickness of the material. If we take wooden material with 0.25 to 0.75 thickness and at Terahertz frequency, we will observe around 14 to 26 DB attenuation. Similarly, for plastic and paper, we will see very large attenuation at higher frequencies. This will directly impact the signal to noise ratio as the higher the path, the higher the penetration loss. So, we will not be able to deliver a signal

with higher signal strength. This results in a lower signal-to-noise ratio, which causes the degradation in signal strength [1].

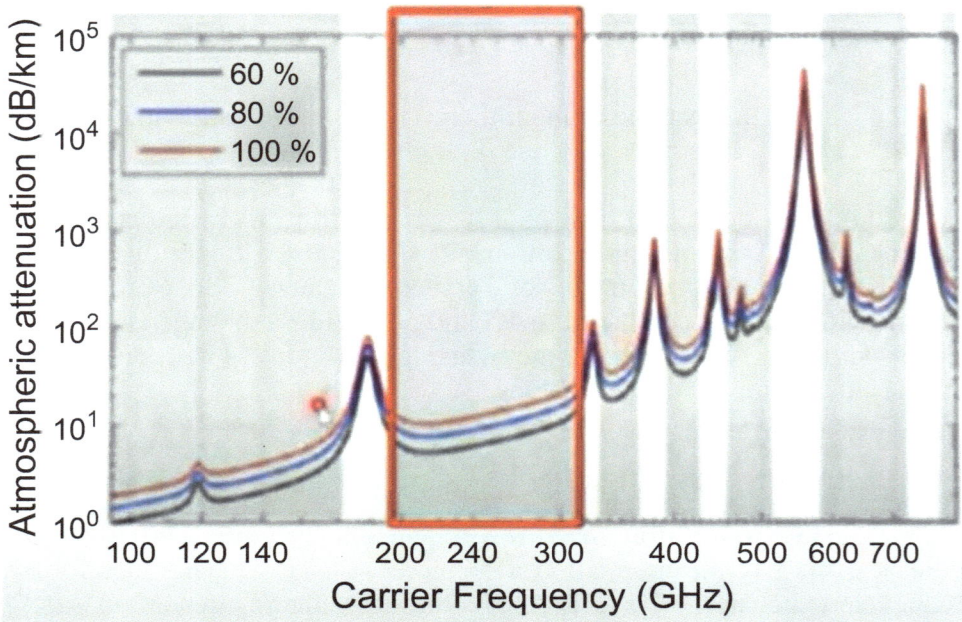

Fig. (1). Attenuation *versus* carrier frequency.

ARCHITECTURE OF 6G

As 6G makes use of Terahertz communication, the architecture of 6G is wider. The wider architecture of Terahertz communication is nothing but the coverage of space, air, ground, and underwater networks. So, all the segments of the communication network come together and work under the same umbrella, framing ubiquitous connectivity so that we can roll across any of the segments easily. The sample architecture of 6G is shown in Fig. (2):

Terahertz communication is intended to be integrated with satellite communications, air networks, and terrestrial and underwater networks. Among this communication, the terrestrial network is the main part, which is the first segment, followed by satellite communication under space. The underwater network is the third segment. All these come together under the same umbrella, forming ubiquitous connectivity. If we look at ubiquitous intelligence in mobile society, there will be different applications of different segments like the IoT segment, sensing as a service segment, environmental sensing, remote monitoring, smart home applications, human-computer interactions, and the vehicle for everything. There are few segments on optical wireless communications or optical fiber cable communications and few segments on satellite communication. All these things come under the same umbrella and frame a ubiquitous, intelligent, mobile society.

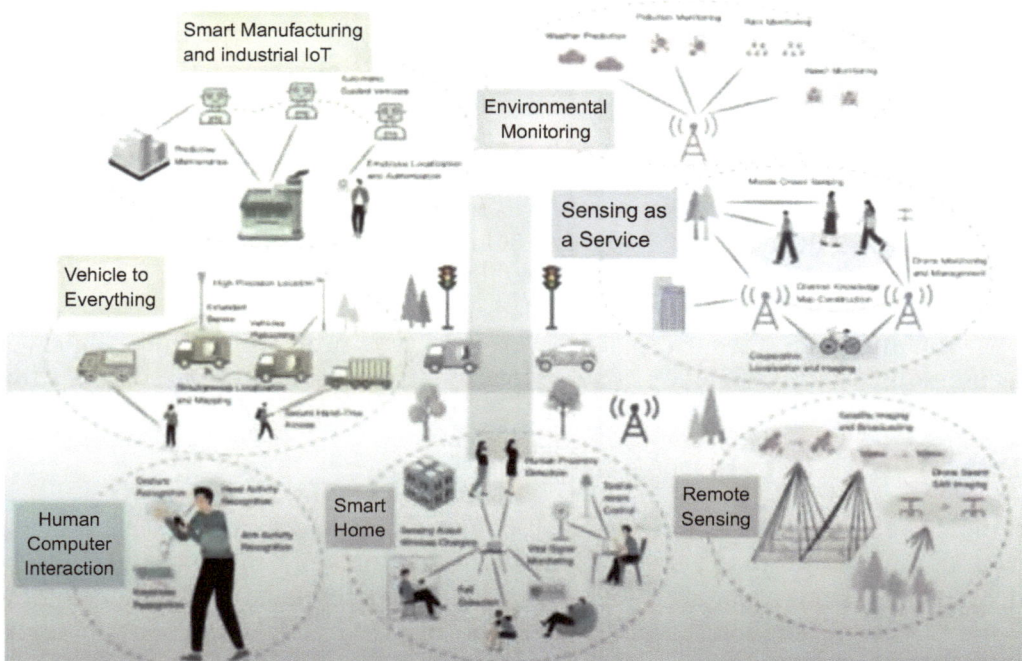

Fig. (2). Architecture of 6G.

POTENTIAL TECHNOLOGIES

i. 6G Test bed: To employ a 6G test bed, we must employ terahertz frequencies, which is a bit challenging because right now, the hardware support is very limited at terahertz communications as the hardware devices need to be operated at much higher frequencies. The vision of 6G communications is to improve the performance of the data rate and latency limitations and permit ubiquitous connectivity. In addition, 6G communications will adopt novel strategies, enabling new communication experiences with virtual existence and universal presence that will be readily available anywhere [2].

ii. Artificial Intelligence and Big Data Analytics: 6G with full integration of AI with big data analytics is required for most real-life applications.

iii. Novel Radio Access Technology: 6G is expected to have the next generation of OFDM, such as Non-Orthogonal Multiple Access (NOMA) technology or a further enhanced version of hybrid NOMA-OFDM, for accessing the radio to improve spectrum utilization with limited power.

iv. Super Massive MIMO(SM-MIMO): To increase the throughput and spectrum efficiency, the supermassive Multiple Input Multiple Output (MIMO) technology needs to be explored.

v. Visible Light Communication (VLC): This is included in 6G architecture as one of the segments people are exploring these days. So, there are a lot of research opportunities under this technology.

vi. Quantum computing: Quantum communication also seems to be a very attractive technology for increasing transmission capabilities by employing qubits instead of traditional bits [2]. It is expected that 6G, as the future mobile cellular system, will benefit from quantum computing, quantum communications, and even quantum sensing. Quantum communication can thus improve 6G security. Although 6G is not yet fully defined, it is expected that QIT (Quantum Information Technology) will be one of the critical enablers. We believe quantum-enabled 6G will bring many advantages, such as quantum-safe security, improved privacy protection, and improved communication efficiency and capacity from quantum-based real-time optimization [3].

RECENT RESEARCH ON 6G AND AI

To meet the challenges ahead, research communities and industry are exploring the sixth generation (6G) Terahertz-based wireless network that is expected to be offered to industrial users in just ten years. Gaining knowledge and understanding of the different challenges and facets of 6G is crucial in meeting future communication requirements and addressing evolving quality of service (QoS) demands. The survey discussed in a study [4] examines specifications, requirements, applications, and enabling technologies related to 6G.

AI and 6G, alongside modern-day technology, have been introduced into healthcare [5] to enhance and innovate the concept of a greater connected and responsive healthcare device. The possible integration of AI and 6G can help healthcare experts and policymakers to establish guidelines and procedures efficiently.

CONCLUDING REMARKS

This chapter provides an overview of 6G technology in terms of the electromagnetic spectrum, architecture, challenges, and potential technologies.

EXERCISES

1. What are the key possibilities for the users of 6G technology?
2. Compare 4G, 5G, and 6G in terms of Terahertz Communication, Haptic Communication, AI Integration, Extended Reality, and Satellite Communication.
3. What are the challenges of 6G wireless communication?
4. What do you mean by Super MIMO technology?
5. Outline the potential technologies of 6G.
6. Demonstrate the architecture of 6G.

REFERENCES

[1] K.K. Vaigandla, "Communication technologies and challenges on 6g networks for the internet: internet of things (iot) based analysis", *IEEE International Conference on Innovative Practices in Technology and Management (ICIPTM)*, 2022.
[http://dx.doi.org/10.1109/ICIPTM54933.2022.9753990]

[2] I. Tomkos, and N.E. Pikasis, *Toward the 6G Network Era: Opportunities and Challenges.* IEEE Computer Society, 2020.

[3] C. Wang, and A. Rahman, *Quantum-Enabled 6G Wireless Networks: Opportunities and Challenges,* 2021.

[4] M.S. Akbar, and Z. Hussain, "On challenges of sixth-generation (6g) wireless networks: A comprehensive survey of requirements, applications, and security issues", *J. Netw. Comput. Appl.,* 2024.

[5] I. Ahmad, Khan1, A. Salam, "Big data analytics model using artificial intelligence (AI) and 6G technologies for healthcare", *IEEE Access*, 2024.

SUBJECT INDEX

A

Ad hoc network 1, 43, 45, 46, 49, 54, 55, 60, 65, 66
Ad Hoc on-demand distance vector routing 63
Advanced mobile phone system (AMPS) 21, 22, 23, 24, 42
Airdrop feature 73
Algorithm 28, 41, 56, 66
  complicated 56
Amplitude 9
  modulation 9
  modulation technique 9
AMPS 22, 24
  channels 22, 24
  network 22
Analog 9, 21
  mobile telephone system (AMTS) 21
  modulation techniques 9
Android smartphones 119
AODV route discovery 64
Apple devices 73
Application(s) 5, 17, 29, 65, 67, 72, 74, 75, 77, 81, 82, 87, 88, 101, 102, 108, 110, 118
  connectivity 17
  industrial 74
  landslide 75
  multidisciplinary 102
  support sublayer (ASS) 108
Applications of WSN 75, 78, 85, 88
  in healthcare 85
  in precision agriculture 88
Architecture of terahertz communication 127, 130
Arduino IDE android smartphone 119
Artificial Intelligence 131
Atmospheric absorption 129
Attenuation, atmospheric 129
AUC Authentication center 27
  and subscriber key 27
  authenticates mobile subscribers 27

Automated electronic triage telemedicine system 87
Automatic teller machines 104

B

Bandwidth 11, 13, 14, 18, 20, 21, 23, 35, 37, 38, 40, 43, 56, 97
  for wireless access based on geographic location 40
  ranging 40
  wastage 11
Beam theorem 97
Big data analytics 131
Bits 18, 22, 29, 40, 41, 51, 111, 131, 132
  digital 41
  guard 29
  synchronization 18
  traditional 132
  training sequence 29
Bluetooth 67, 68, 69, 70, 71, 72, 73, 75, 77, 101, 102, 105, 106, 114, 115, 119
  adapters 68
  and transferring files 73
  applications 72, 114
  communication 71
  connections 115
  devices 70, 71, 115
  low energy (BLE) 105, 119
  network 69
  security 72, 115
  technologies 72, 75, 114
  wireless connection 115
BPSK and QPSK modulation techniques 75
Broadband wireless access (BWA) 50
Building sensor networks 80
Business activities 103

C

CDMA 18, 31, 33
  applications 33

9798898810146